JESUS UNBRANDED
VOLUME 1
STORIES WITHOUT SPIN

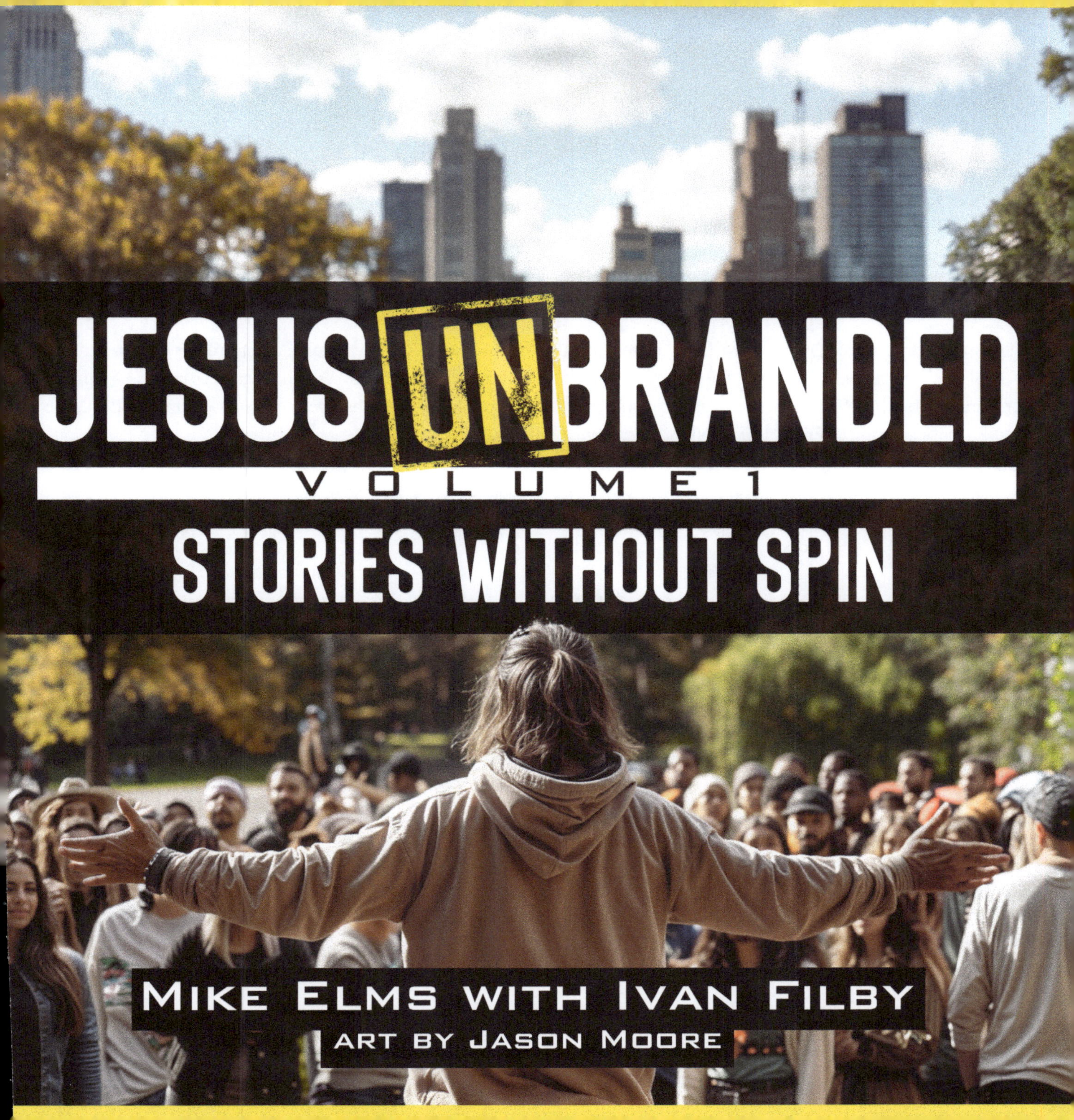

JESUS UN BRANDED

VOLUME 1

STORIES WITHOUT SPIN

MIKE ELMS WITH IVAN FILBY

ART BY JASON MOORE

Jesus Unbranded: Volume One
Stories Without Spin

ISBN 978-1-9632-6531-6

24 25 26 27 28 29 30 31 32 33—10 9 8 7 6 5 4 3 2 1

MANUFACTURED in the UNITED STATES of AMERICA

Contents

Jesus unbranded: volume two
Stories with bite

. . . .

The parables

Lost (and found)
- The missing pupil
- The lost wedding ring
- The tale of the teenage wastrel

(Lost) and found

Travellers' tales
- The sassy theme park manager
- The two landlords
- The laborers on the building site
- The referee's tale
- Sparring on the stump
- The store managers

Travellers' tales told

Meek, mild, as if...
- A tale of two plumbers
- The rebellious board
- The big game

...Meek, mild, as if

Where do you stand?
- Tales of the expected
- The impatient paparazzi
- A shanty of sailboats and motorboats

Where do you stand?

Foreword | Let's keep the stories alive

It was a Sunday in Meopham, a small village in southeast England, an hour's drive from London.

The autumnal sunshine was lancing through the windows of the small Baptist chapel.

Dust motes pirouetted in the sunbeams as the Pastor read Matthew 22:1-14: The parable of the Wedding Banquet.

I looked at the faces around me and saw many blank expressions.

A number had closed eyes, but closed in vexation, rather than meditation.

Some younger eyes were downcast.

Cast downwards onto their mobile phone.

But onto YouTube, rather than YouVersion.

All the signs of a disengaged congregation.

The Pastor finished the reading and picked up the notes of his sermon.

I thought to myself: *"Your congregation has lost interest before you've even started."*

I recalled that this parable was the final part of a trilogy of parables Jesus told during Holy Week. It followed hard on the heels of the parables of the Tenants and the Two Sons.

All three were told in public spaces. Together, they formed a scathing attack on the religious authorities in Jerusalem. Their meaning to the authorities and the crowd would have been clear. The authorities would have been furious, the crowd delighted.

One thing was for sure. No one there would have been disengaged or disinterested.

Jesus never, ever, bored people.

And then I thought: *Guinness.*

At that time, I was CEO of a big ad agency in London with a long list of blue-chip clients including Ford, American Express, Unilever, Shell, Nestlé, Microsoft, and Reebok.

And Guinness, which in Adland, is iconic. The brand had been built upon several decades worth of cutting-edge advertising, but those ads had failed to move with the times and were now failing to enthuse its consumers.

While a brand can survive many things, it cannot survive irrelevance and indifference.

So, Guinness was in poor shape. Marginalized. Struggling.

Our challenge was to put the sparkle back into its ads, to put Guinness back on its prestigious advertising pedestal. And, by so doing, to connect the brand with a whole new audience.

We did so by casting Rutger Hauer as "The Man with the Guinness," who ruminated on life, the universe, and everything, underscored by the tagline, "Guinness, Pure Genius."

The campaign was idiosyncratic, bemusing, challenging.

It was applauded by some and derided by others.

It intrigued some and baffled others.

What people were not, was disinterested. What the ads were not was ignored. The campaign created interest and debate. It got people talking.

It didn't change the brand. It took it back to its roots. Reaffirmed it. Revitalized it.

(At that time, our family lived in an Edwardian country house. When first built in 1901 it was at the cutting edge of technology. It had electricity! But 100 years later, the electrical system was obsolete. So, we had it rewired. The house was once again fit for purpose.)

Guinness was back center stage. Rewired. Once again fit for purpose.

Today the brand name alone is valued at over $2 billion dollars.

The essence of great advertising is that it is cutting-edge.

It has to cut through. To cut through media noise, and to cut into people's minds.

"Just do it!"

"Finger Lickin' Good"

"Where's the beef?"

"Don't leave home without it!"

Catch my drift? (Not an ad campaign, but it could be!)

The parables Jesus told had real "cut-through."

He knew his audiences, he knew the culture, he knew the messaging he wanted to convey, and he constructed his storylines accordingly.

Some entertained, some shocked, some challenged, some affirmed.

But all connected with their audiences and conveyed the underlying messaging that Jesus wanted to get across.

Jesus never, ever, bored people.

Finally, I thought: *Jesus may have been a carpenter, but he'd have also made a great adman!*

I recalled that I was taught in my earliest days as an adman that the golden rule in advertising is to stand in the shoes of your audience, to see things from their perspective and communicate accordingly.

I think maybe that's one of the reasons why Jesus came to us, as one of us.

As the Pastor started unpacking the parable, I sat back to try to concentrate.

However, yet another thought came to mind. But this one wasn't my thought. Unbidden, this one was livestreamed into my brain:

Mike, the culture of your society, here and today, is very different from the one I preached into 2000 years ago. The stories I told then don't connect and resonate in the same way now.

I could see that by looking at the faces around me. Storylines woven around Samaritans, virgins with lamps, fig trees, Pharisees, vineyards, and three thousand litres of olive oil don't have the sort of impact now as they had when first told in first-century Palestine.

Mike, use your skills to create new storylines that will refresh the Parables brand. Tell them the way you think I'd tell them, here and now. Stand in my shoes, as I stand in their shoes. Keep the messaging the same but make the stories relevant. Give them cut-through. Make them fit for purpose. Rewire them!

I balked at this: "Lord, I'm not a theologian, I'm an adman."

Mike, that's exactly why I'm giving this task to you.

As a committed Christian and as a seasoned adman, I knew I had been given a Mission:
"Keep my stories alive."

Then God sent Ivan my way, a man full of the Spirit and theology and keen to join with me on that Mission. And so we set to work.

And then he sent Jason to join us. Very Trinitarian!

Mike Elms
London, 2024

Wired | Stories that carry power

Most of us can recall an outstanding teacher
from our schooldays:

par·a·ble(s)
an earthly story
with a spiritual truth

A teacher with a passion for their subject and for us.

A teacher with great wisdom.

A teacher with a unique teaching style.

A teacher that made us want to learn.

A teacher that left an indelible mark on our lives.

Jesus was all this and more:

A brilliant teacher who also happened to be the Son of God.

A teacher in whom two worlds intersected, the spiritual and the physical, heaven and earth.

At the heart of his teaching lie the parables.

Stories that he created and related in his own words.

Stories that he told to reconcile his two perspectives.

Stories that use familiar, everyday settings to convey eternal, spiritual themes.

Stories that we can understand and from which we can learn life-changing truths.

To spend time with the parables is to spend time with Jesus, with his disciples, with the crowds that followed him, and even with the authorities that opposed him.

To spend time with the parables enables us to see and engage with the spiritual themes that permeate the events, relationships, and situations in our everyday lives.

The lives that we are living, here and today.

Rewired | When is a tablet not a tablet?

Jesus was passionate about getting his message across.

We can see his frustration as even his closest followers struggled to get it:

You of little faith, why are you talking among yourselves about having no bread? Do you still not understand.... How is it you don't understand that I was not talking to you about bread? (Matthew 16: 8-9,11)

To remedy their lack of understanding, Jesus used props and storylines drawn from everyday life.

Things that were culturally relevant.

Stories that true faith-seekers could understand and relate to.

This begs a question: If Jesus were telling these stories to us today, here and now, would he not realize that we are unfamiliar with the way of life of a first-century, Middle Eastern agricultural society?

Of course, he would. So, surely, he would create and relate stories rooted in the 21st-century?

In the Americas, Europe, Asia, Africa, Oceania, he'd find similar cultural touchpoints, so keen is he that all grasp his message and have an opportunity to respond to his claims.

He would draw upon modern-day commerce, entertainment, media, technology, sports, medicine, and social protocols, and he would use them as physical, everyday analogies and storylines to communicate his eternal, spiritual themes.

He would keep the themes and messaging of the stories unchanged.

But he would wire his words into today's world.

This thought first struck Mike in the closing years of the last century. It gave birth to the rewiring of the "Good Samaritan" as the *"Compassionate Millwall fan."* (In the United Kingdom, fans of the Millwall soccer team are not noted for their sociability, gentleness of disposition, or considerate behavior towards others![1])

. . . .

[1]Perhaps like a Philadelphia Eagles fan today.—The Publisher (who is also a Dallas Cowboys fan).

One Sunday he preached on it.

People told him that it worked well, and they encouraged him to write more.

So, he did. This led him to write a short sermon series, after which, he could feel God nudging him to write still more. Eventually, he realized he was being nudged to rewire all of the parables.

At first, Mike resisted the nudge. He didn't have the time. He had too many marketing consultancy projects. He had a family, and he was training for marathons.

Plus, it felt like an intimidating challenge. Jesus told a lot of parables.

But the nudge became an increasingly more forceful shove.

God simply shut down his marketing projects.

Mike and his wife, Valerie, became empty nesters.

He soon realized that he would not better his 3h 43m marathon in Chicago.

Eventually, he capitulated and sat down at his keyboard.

Closed his eyes and prayed.

Opened his spirit and wrote.

Then Ivan joined the party.

Ivan met Mike at an event at the House of Lords. They chatted about their writing projects, and Mike handed Ivan a copy of *Parables: Rewired* in a brown paper envelope! Rightly so: Jesus' parables are dangerous stuff.

Ivan read them all in one sitting at Heathrow Airport and laughed out loud.

Then, he read them again, one by one, in many sittings.

One day in a phone conversation, Ivan threw out the challenge: "Mike, you need to rewire your book of parables for our friends in North America. I can help if you like."

Mike liked. And so, the Good Samaritan became the "Caring Russian Ultra," and together we developed a method of working.

Our first task was to identify the main message Jesus sought to communicate.

That had to be respected and protected at all costs.

We've submitted our work to eminent theologians to check that we have achieved this. They say we have. We pray that they are right.

The parables often contain sub-themes, which we suspect were not Jesus' main thrust or even intent, but which, as so often is the case in storytelling, grew unbidden out of the storyline. We set out to identify these and, where possible, bring them out in our rewiring.

We think we've been reasonably successful but not universally so. Sometimes it has proved impossible to replicate all of the first-century cultural analogies entirely.

On the other hand, some sub-themes have emerged from our own storytelling. Where we are conscious that this is the case, we have checked them against Jesus' teaching. If they have stood scrutiny, we have let them remain.

For instance, you'll see that we have used a ski slope white-out in our rewiring of the Lost Sheep. When Mike preached on the story, a keen skier in the congregation said the concept transfixed her. In a white-out, she said, you feel isolated, afraid, and terribly alone. The retelling had helped her see the parable from the sheep's perspective, lost in a spiritual white-out.

We had not spotted this, and it's entirely likely that there are other sub-messages that we have not spotted. As you read these stories, they may speak a message peculiar to you and to you alone. If so, listen hard, because it's not from us: it's God speaking directly to you.

Finally, and crucially, we must stress that we have rewired the parables to supplement the originals, not to replace them, which is why we have also included the stories as Jesus himself told them.

We happily acknowledge that Jesus was a far better storyteller than we are!

Hotwired | Instructions for use

This is a resource book.

When you read it make sure you have a pen in your hand and use it, liberally.

Cross out what you don't agree with. Underline what you do.

Amend. Annotate.

Don't feel a need to read the whole book in one go. Take your time. Take as much time to read it as it has taken us to write it. Hint: that's a lot of time. As you read, have a cup of tea or coffee. Read it by yourself. Then maybe discuss it over a meal with some friends. That's very biblical and exactly what the original hearers may have done.

Each parable follows the same format:

Rewiring

As we've said, the themes and messaging of the parables are timeless, but the storylines are time limited. The product is terrific, but the packaging is perhaps a little dated. Imagine a world without teabags or without squeezable honey and mayonnaise, a world of hard unspreadable butter, milk only in glass bottles. You might be saying: "Oh, yes please," in which case you may like this next part.

Reminding

After each 'rewiring', we've included the original parable. It's in the NIV translation. Sorry if that's not your bag. There's always Bible Gateway!

Resetting and retelling happen a lot. Think about Joe Cocker's cover of the Beatles' *With a Little Help from My Friends* or the remake of *The Italian Job*.

On just about every episode of *America's Got Talent* or *The Voice*, you'll hear new interpretations of old classics.

And, shocker, Bradley Cooper's and Lady Gaga's 2018 movie, *A Star is Born*, is also a remake of the 1954 release, itself a reinterpretation of the original release from 1937.

People retell stories, remake movies, or rerecord songs to keep them relevant and alive.

We're both Shakespeare junkies. Consequently, we've seen many productions that reset his plays in a modern setting. Often, they add fresh angles, which expand and enrich our experience. But invariably, we find ourselves cross-referring back to the original text. It's great to hold the two in tension.

That's another reason why we've included the original parables.

Interpretation

Occasionally the Gospels show Jesus having to explain his parables to his audience. Given that the audience who didn't get it often included the people who wrote or inspired the Gospels, we suspect that Jesus had to explain his stories more times than they cared to record!

This knowledge brought us to the tricky bit.

Our original intention was to just rewire the stories and let the audience take it from there. But our friends urged us not to do that. They said it would be a complete cop-out. They pushed us to draw out some messaging and implications, and 'hotwire' them to us, here and now.

Mike's an adman, not an ordained clergyman, and does not have a degree in theology. But as an ad man, Mike knows how to get a message across. This has equipped him to become an experienced preacher.

Ivan however is an ordained minister with deep theological insight. He also has a ton of training in business. This has equipped him to become an experienced professor, dean, and university president.

Together, we've found, we make a great team.

Even so, look on our 'hotwiring thoughts' as a starter for ten. If they are helpful, great—build on them. If they're not, please feel free to ignore them.

But, either way, do take time to think about what the parable (original, rewired, or as we strongly suggest, the two together) may be saying to you here and now.

Reflection

Jesus was the consummate teacher. When he wasn't telling stories, he was asking questions.

We like both approaches.

So, we've also posed some questions which we've had the temerity to upgrade and call "Reflections."

Response

This section is always blank, as we have nothing to say here, because this is all about you. What you think and say is as important as anything we've written in this book.

As authors, we know how intimidating a blank section can be. But we encourage you to try and write something, anything.

Look at it as a letter to Jesus.

That's what we did and look at where it has led us.

Where to start

Many authors say that the first page is the most difficult, that their brain suddenly becomes as blank as the page or screen.

But that's about *how* to start, and that wasn't our problem.

We were presented with umpteen parables. Potential storylines were firing our brains, not freezing them.

No, our problem was *where* to start. Which parable should be first, and what should be the order thereafter?

In our first draft, we decided to take things in biblical order: start with the parables recorded by Matthew, then onto Mark, and finally sweep up with Luke. (John wasn't big on parables!) Then we were struck by a Big Idea. How about putting them into chronological order?

Great idea.

Bad idea.

We rapidly discovered that biblical chronology is fraught with challenges. We knew that was the case with the Old Testament, but surely the New Testament would be a lot easier, particularly the Gospels. Nope. For instance, we discovered that John's Gospel is the only one that makes it clear that Jesus' ministry spanned three years. Matthew, Mark, and Luke were more concerned with recording what happened, rather than when and in what order.

So, there are mismatches within and across the Gospels. Theologians of infinitely greater eminence than we have helpfully put forward varying suggestions on sequencing, which then, unhelpfully, differ.

It became clear to us that coming up with a chronology of Jesus' ministry and then inserting the parables within that was the theological equivalent of the search for the Holy Grail. Like Lancelot and Indiana Jones, we persevered. Our research offered several interpretations. All we had to do was choose one. But which one?

One, in particular, stood out, because it listed the first parable to be told as new wine into old wineskins and the last as sheep and goats. This meant that Jesus' first parable was about wine and told at the same time as his first miracle at the wedding in Cana, which was also all about wine. Both the parable and the miracle presaged the beginning of his ministry. That worked for us. It also meant that his last parable was about his second coming and Judgement Day. That also worked for us.

In fact, we became incredibly excited because we were seeing the parables in a new way: in the light of Jesus' ministry.

Chronology

Timeline of Jesus' ministry

AD 26

Summer • Baptism

• Wilderness temptations

Autumn • First miracle: water into wine

AD 27

Winter • Cleansing of the Temple

Summer • Andrew, Peter, James and John join

Autumn • Matthew joins

AD 28

Winter • Jesus chooses the 12 disciples

• Woman at the well

Spring • Sermon on the Mount

Summer • Travel through Galilee

Autumn • Calming the storm; disciples sent out

AD 29

Winter • Feeding of the 5000

Spring • Walks on water

Summer • Transfiguration

Autumn • Raising of Lazarus

AD 30

Winter • Journey to Jerusalem

• Healing of blind Bartimaeus

Spring • Visit to Martha and Mary

• Palm Sunday

• Cleansing of the Temple

• Last Supper, arrest and crucifixion

• Resurrection

Timeline of the parables

1 • New cloth and new wine

2-3 • Lamp under bushel > wise and foolish builders

4-9 • Debtors and creditor > sower

10-17 • 'Heaven is' series

18-19 • Master and servant > unmerciful servant

20-21 • Good Samaritan > Friend in need

22-24 • Places of honour > counting the cost

25-33 • 'Lost and found' series; shrewd steward > talents

34-36 • 'Meek, mild, as if' series

37-39 • 'Where do you stand?' series

Stories without spin

We decided to publish this book as two volumes for two reasons.

The first was practical.

There are, in total, 39 different parables recorded across the Gospels of Matthew, Mark and Luke. We decided to create a couple of 'combi-parables', but that still left 37. By the time we had rewired them, included the originals, added a commentary and reflection, left space and time for reader input, and then added art; we realized we were looking at a very large book! Too large.

The second reason was spiritual.

You'll see that our chronology has Jesus telling parables in a ministry that lasted a little over three years. (That matches what most historians believe, although there are some who would contend it was just one year. But, hey, this is our book and we're going to side with the majority!)

Once we had placed all the parables in the context of Jesus' ministry, we could see very clearly that they divided into two types with two different purposes.

Jesus spent most of the first three years of his ministry travelling around Galilee and surrounding areas, (including brief visits to Jerusalem, depending on how one interprets the various and varying Gospel timelines).

The tone of the parables he told was engaging, surprising, sometimes light-hearted, other times shocking, and always illuminating.

These were *'teaching parables'*.

'Stories without spin'.

Then, late in the third year, the winter of AD 29/30 Jesus 'set his face toward Jerusalem' and the climax of his ministry.

The tone of the parables he told during this period was massively different. They were urgent, darker, gloves-off, and politically super-charged.

These were *'preaching parables'*.

'Stories with bite'.

This first volume, *Jesus Unbranded: Stories Without Spin*, focuses on the teaching parables, which we have grouped into three series.

The first series, *'Listen Up,'* comprises 9 parables.

We were initially surprised to find a year's gap between first and second parables. But then we realized that, during that time, Jesus was finding his feet and gathering his disciples. So, the second and third parables, the lamp under the bushel and the wise and foolish builders, came as the culmination of his first major teaching session, the Sermon on the Mount, and formed a powerful injunction to his new adherents to pay heed to what he had said.

The parables that follow build upon the Sermon on the Mount as Jesus teaches people the importance of living their lives forgivingly, generously, expectantly, faithfully, and fruitfully.

The concluding parable, the Sower, is told before the disciples are sent out to spread the word.

The *'Heaven Is'* series of parables accompanies the sending out of the disciples on their preaching mission and, in effect, says: 'Here's the message I want you to get across'.

The eight stories Jesus told (two of which we have presented as two-parters) is an invaluable coaching session to the disciples (and us) on how to talk engagingly about God's Kingdom, the 'Kingdom of Heaven'.

Finally, in the *'Mark My Words'* series of seven stories, Jesus emphasises more of the themes from the Sermon on the Mount, with instruction on how to live our lives dutifully, mercifully, compassionately, prayerfully, with humility, thankfully, and committedly.

The second volume of *Jesus Unbranded* focuses upon the 'preaching parables' and traces the dramatic events up to and into Jerusalem, during which Jesus takes a gloves-off approach to his story-telling. An approach which was to cost him his life…

The parables volume one | Stories without spin

Rewired	Original
Listen up	
When new into old won't go	New cloth and new wine
The farewell tour and the Ferrari	Lamp under the bushel
The astute and reckless investors	Wise and foolish builders
A tale of two punters	Debtors and creditor
The selfish lawyer	Rich fool
The story of the night watch	Alert servants
The tale of the CEO's dilemma	Faithful steward
The failing project	Fig tree without figs
The reluctant advertiser	Sower
Listening up	
Heaven is...	
Junk mail	Weeds
The retirement fund	Growing seed
Look up and look in	Mustard seed and yeast
The nickel and the carp	Hidden treasure and the pearl
The job applications	Net
The wine merchant	Owner of the house
...Heaven is	
Mark my words	
The tale of the two drivers	Master and his servant
The case of the vindictive landlord	Unmerciful servant
The caring Russian Ultra	Good Samaritan
The panicking colleague	Friend in need
A dramatic night at the Oscars	Places of honor at the wedding feast
The free lunch	Great banquet
The tale of the no-good do-gooders	Counting the cost
Marked by his words	

LISTEN UP!

(THE SHOW'S ABOUT TO START)

These are the early parables and, as they unfold, we can see Jesus developing his story-telling skills.

The stories captivated and challenged their audiences in equal measure.

From the curtain-opening New Cloth and New Wine; to the dramatic Wise and Foolish Builders; and onto the chilling tale of the Rich Fool.

We are told that people were amazed because *'he taught as one who has authority, and not as their teachers of the law'* (Matthew 7:29).

Jesus had come to bring new teaching and to teach it in a radically different style.

We see that style evolving as this series of stories progresses, culminating in the seminal Parable of the Sower.

At the end of which he throws out a challenge to his audience:

'Whoever has ears to hear, let them hear' (Mark 4:9).

A challenge that he was to repeat on more than one occasion.

So, as you read these stories, imagine Jesus telling them to you, along with that same challenge:

'Pin back your ears, and listen up!'

TWO TALES OF WHEN NEW INTO OLD WON'T GO

A much-loved car...in a very sorry state.
Can it be given a new lease on life?

While Jesus was having a meal at Matthew's house, some of John the Baptist's followers came to ask him why he and his disciples did not follow the old rules about fasting. As was his wont, Jesus replied with some stories and questions:

· ·

I took my car to the auto repair shop the other day.

It's a classic 1970 Shelby Ford Mustang in candy apple red that my grandfather left to me in his estate. He stored it in his barn for years, and the bodywork is now pretty shabby. But I love the car, and it reminds me of Gramps, so I wanted to know whether the repair shop could source and fit it with another body shell.

"I could probably dig up a body shell somewhere," the mechanic said, "But the chassis is completely rusted, and there's no way it will support a new body shell. It would simply fall apart."

"Well, OK, how about just fitting a new engine?" I replied, somewhat downcast, "This one has done 200,000 miles."

The mechanic laughed. "I can certainly find you a new engine, but do you really want me to do that? If I put it in, the whole car will disintegrate the first time you drive it!"

"What you need is a new engine with a new chassis and body shell. It will set you back a bit, but that way, you'll still have your beloved Mustang, and it will be fit for future use."

"What would you guys have done?"

• •

The next day I called an electrician out to my house. "I'd like you to install a state-of-the-art electronic security system," I said.

"Yep, I could do that, but why bother? Your panel board isn't updated enough. The system would constantly be tripping."

"Well, in that case, let's just fit a separate circuit breaker," I replied, somewhat smugly, deploying the entirety of my limited electrical lexicon.

I received a pitying look. "Do you really want me to do that? If I do, I'll need to re-wire the whole house, as you'll have fuses popping faster than champagne corks at a wedding. That's if the house hasn't burnt down first.

"You need to re-wire, fit a new panel board, and then install the security system. It won't be cheap, but it will make your house fit for future purpose."

"Again, what would you guys have done?"

The parable of new cloth and new wine

Matthew 9:16-17

[16]"No one sews a patch of un-shrunk cloth on an old garment, for the patch will pull away from the garment, making the tear worse. [17]Neither do people pour new wine into old wineskins. If they do, the skins will burst; the wine will run out and the wine-skins will be ruined. No, they pour new wine into new wineskins, and both are preserved."

Luke 5:36-38

[36]He told them this parable, "No one tears a piece out of a new garment to patch an old one. Otherwise, they will have torn the new garment, and the patch from the new will not match the old. [37]And no one pours new wine into old wineskins. Otherwise, the new wine will burst the skins; the wine will run out and the wineskins will be ruined. [38]No, new wine must be poured into new wineskins."

Mark 2:21-22

[21]"No one sews a patch of un-shrunk cloth on an old garment. Otherwise, the new piece will pull away from the old, making the tear worse. [22]And no one pours new wine into old wineskins. Otherwise, the wine will burst the skins, and both the wine and the wineskins will be ruined. No, they pour new wine into new wine-skins."

So, what's this story saying to US, here and now?

This short and enigmatic story is Jesus' first parable, told at the very beginning of his ministry.

Around the same time, Jesus was also performing his first miracle at the wedding in Cana. So, in a perfect piece of divine symmetry, his first parable and his first miracle both involve wine, and both point towards the culmination of his ministry with the cup of wine at the Last Supper.

Nothing Jesus did or said was ever anything less than deeply significant.

In that vein, at the very outset of his ministry, Jesus told this parable to make the point that he had come to do new things in a new way and that people should not expect him to be subject to, or conform to, old traditions.

Things they were a-changing.

As we all know, change can be an uncomfortable and threatening process, but it can also be exciting and revitalising.

The best way to deal with change is to approach it in the yet-to-be story of the future rather than closed-book history of the past. What and where is it leading to? What are the challenges and opportunities it will create?

As Jesus himself said: *"Do not think that I have come to abolish the Law or the Prophets; I have not come to abolish them but to fulfill them"* (Matthew 5:17).

When we accept Jesus into our lives, he will change us. Some of that change will be uncomfortable. But, if we embrace it, Jesus will change the whole of our character and our life for the better.

We will emerge from the process not just as a renovation but as a completely new creation, fit for future purpose and an eternal future at that.

Wow! Doesn't that leave us wanting to hear more stories?

Which is why Jesus told this story as his first parable.

Reflection and prayer | Am I fit for future purpose?

. . . .

What's this story saying to **me,** here and now?

. . . .

THE FAREWELL TOUR AND THE FERRARI

A mega rock star...and a dream machine.
Could they be denied center stage?

Jesus' first recorded piece of extended preaching was the *Sermon on the Mount*, which starts with the *Beatitudes:* a series of eight blessings that set out the standards Jesus requires from us for spiritual living and the consequent benefits. (The rest of the sermon outlines how these spiritual standards should also shape our behaviors, and we'll explore this in the next parable.) At the end of the *Beatitudes*, Jesus issued a challenge to his followers, which naturally he couldn't resist illustrating with a story or two:

· ·

Your mission is to be an example to the world. Take it seriously...

When Elton John played his *Yellow Brick Road* farewell concert in New York, did he perform his first gig in a small bar on Seventh Avenue?

No! He kicked it off by playing Madison Square Garden. Twice.

The parable of the lamp under the bushel

Matthew
5:14-16

When Ferrari launches a new model, do they invite a couple of local press journalists to a sandwich lunch in a back-street garage?

No! They build a massive and very glitzy stand at the Geneva Motor Show and fly in the world's media to see the car unveiled by a Hollywood superstar.

14 "You are the light of the world. A town built on a hill cannot be hidden. 15 Neither do people light a lamp and put it under a bowl. Instead they put it on its stand, and it gives light to everyone in the house. 16 In the same way, let your light shine before others, that they may see your good deeds and glorify your Father in heaven."

So, what's this story saying to US, here and now?

Centuries ago, Christianity dominated the arts scene in the Western world.

Music, art, poetry, architecture, sculpture—the vast majority of the classic works were created to be in praise of God.

The Christian theme was a shining beacon. Churches were built on hills with steeples and towers so they could be seen from miles around.

These days, Christian literature is confined to less than half an aisle in Barnes and Noble. There are more famous paintings of cultural celebrities than biblical characters. Outside of Christian radio, seldom does a Christian-themed song get any airplay, let alone make the charts, even at Christmas.

It's hard for us, individually, to do much about this.

But how visible are we, individually, as Christians? Yes, it's great that we go to church, but most of the rest of the world doesn't see us there.

Only 20% of Americans are active Christians. Here's what they look like on a Sunday:

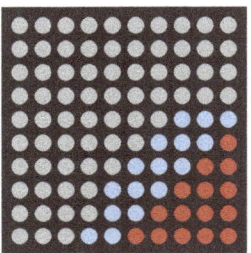

But here's what they look like during the rest of the week:

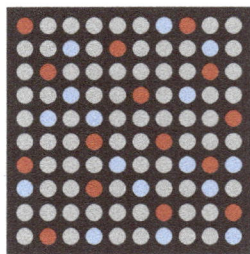

The question for us, as individuals, is how do we make our faith, and Christ, visible to our families, neighbors, friends, colleagues, and acquaintances? It's the challenge Jesus issued to his disciples, and it's the challenge he is giving to you and us here and now.

Reflection and prayer | How bright is my light?

· ·

_____

_____

_____

_____

_____

What's this story saying to me, here and now?

· ·

_____

_____

_____

_____

_____

THE ASTUTE AND
RECKLESS INVESTORS

One follows his head...
the other follows a whim.

To conclude the Sermon on the Mount, Jesus told this parable to emphasize how important it was that people acted upon what he was saying:

· ·

The late 1980s were an incredible time to be working in financial services. This was the time of yuppy-mania: young guns toting the new-fangled mobile phones, tearing around in the latest Corvette, and making five or six-figure bonuses.

At the end of 1988, two such types—Hamza and Wei—each picked up a $150,000 year-end bonus. Neither needed a new Corvette, each decided their 45-foot powerboat was big enough, and both had had two Caribbean holidays that year. But while they qualified as conspicuous consumers, they were also savvy enough to realize that the good times might not run forever. Therefore, they each decided to invest their latest windfalls to provide greater security in the longer term. Each decided he would buy a business.

But what?

Hamza, always impetuous, was typically quick off the mark. He was clear about the sort of business he wanted to buy. It needed to satisfy two criteria. First, it had to be something he would get excited about—fashion and glamor being top of the list. Second, it had to provide a quick return on his investment. He found exactly what he was after in the form of a luxury car import dealership. He quickly did the deal, not even bothering to negotiate down the sale price (even though, at half a million dollars, it was more than three times his original intended investment).

Wei also had just two criteria. But he showed himself to be more cautious, and arguably, a little cannier than Hamza. For him, a glamor product and big short-term rewards were not the issues. The business he was after would need to display a sound business model and offer long-term growth potential. He identified three companies, did extensive due diligence on each, and eventually bought a small chain of shops in Tennessee selling budget-priced DIY materials.

For a while, all was fine. Wei's discount DIY chain did steady business, and Hamza's Japanese import dealership boomed.

Then the situation changed. High-interest rates and poor exchange rates increased the costs of bought-in goods—especially imports. Wage demands started to spiral. Finally, real disaster struck as the chill wind of recession whooshed throughout the country, blowing pink slips left, right, and center.

Hamza's business crashed. He found himself with large stocks of luxury cars with no one to buy them and half a dozen high-salaried salesmen demanding to be looked after one way or another. The arithmetic simply wouldn't work, and the whole show collapsed around him, leaving him owing hundreds of thousands of dollars. With no job in Wall Street (he'd been let go), he was forced to declare bankruptcy.

Wei had also been made redundant from his Wall Street job. But the homework he'd done on his business investment now paid off. His business plan provided a firm foundation in these more challenging times. The demand for reasonably priced DIY materials held up as people put off moving into new homes and opted to remodel their current ones instead. His staff accepted a pay freeze linked to a promise of catch-up bonuses when things improved. The basic economics and cashflow of his business were sound. He found that it grew through this period of adversity. He gave his friend Hamza a job as a delivery driver. Over time, he was able to reward his staff and expand the business. It went from strength to strength, and his small DIY chain is now a large nationwide company.

And Hamza is his Transport and Logistics Director.

The parable of the wise and foolish builders

Matthew
7:24-29

Luke
6:47-49

24 "Therefore everyone who hears these words of mine and puts them into practice is like a wise man who built his house on the rock. 25The rain came down, the streams rose, and the winds blew and beat against that house; yet it did not fall, because it had its foundation on the rock. 26But everyone who hears these words of mine and does not put them into practice is like a foolish man who built his house on sand. 27The rain came down, the streams rose, and the winds blew and beat against that house, and it fell with a great crash."

28When Jesus had finished saying these things, the crowds were amazed at his teaching, 29because he taught as one who had authority, and not as their teachers of the law.

47 "As for everyone who comes to me and hears my words and puts them into practice, I will show you what they are like. 48They are like a man building a house, who dug down deep and laid the foundation on rock. When a flood came, the torrent struck that house but could not shake it, because it was well built. 49But the one who hears my words and does not put them into practice is like a man who built a house on the ground without a foundation. The moment the torrent struck that house, it collapsed and its destruction was complete."

So, what's this story saying to US, here and now?

Jesus' original parable is almost self-evident. What builder wouldn't build on solid ground? It's obvious, isn't it?

So, it may be helpful to think about why Jesus told the parable.

As we've pointed out, it comes as the concluding element of the Sermon on the Mount, Jesus' first recorded piece of extended preaching. It's a long sermon occupying three chapters of Matthew's Gospel, and it's well worth reading through in one go.

The Sermon is challenging and calls people to a higher moral and ethical living standard. So high that many scholars have dismissed it as being unrealistic. Others argue that that is the very point. The only way we can get anywhere near these standards is with the help of Jesus.

All of this makes this parable really important because Jesus uses it as a call to us to base our lives on his words, his teaching. It's a call to action. The people who heard it at the time were amazed at the authority with which he spoke. Unlike the prevaricating teachers of the law, Jesus was a man who dealt in certainties.

The point remains that our reaction to the parable may well be, "Why on earth wouldn't a builder put his house on rock?"

But that's so often the way with Jesus' words and teaching. When we read it, it seems absolutely inarguable. The trouble comes when we try to put it into practice. It's not easy. In fact, it's really, really, difficult. The temptation then is to shift bits of that teaching onto some sandy ground that may be a bit easier. In Hamza's case, into a business that produces a faster buck, albeit with higher risk.

And we may also have the serpent hissing into our ear: *"Did Jesus really say…?"*

Even with Jesus helping us, it can be a struggle. Without him, it's impossible.

This is a parable about faith. Building our faith upon the rock that is Jesus, putting our complete and absolute trust in him.

Reflection and prayer | What do I want to build on my rock?

. . . .

_____

_____

_____

_____

_____

_____

What's this story saying to **me,** here and now?

. . . .

_____

_____

_____

_____

_____

_____

A TALE OF
TWO PUNTERS

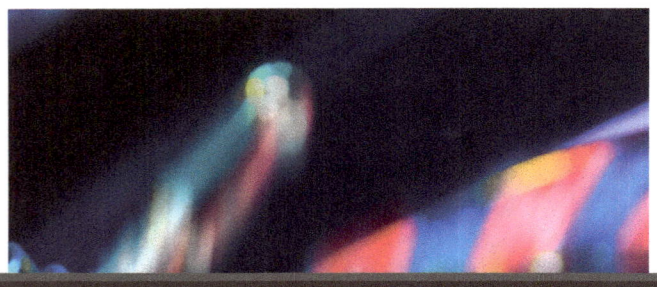

Both get in over their heads...
one much deeper than the other.

ote: A "punter" is British slang for someone who engages in a small but high-odds bet in the hopes of making a quick, lucrative payout.—ed.

Jesus looked at the man before him: "Simon, I'm going to tell you a story."

"Well, if you insist," came the reply.

"Yes, I do."

. . . .

Linda and Valerie worked as hospice nurses in the UK near the White Cliffs of Dover.

They would be the first to admit that the pay wasn't great, but they were able to get by. And, like many hospice nurses, they saw it as a vocation as much as a job.

But it was emotionally demanding, so whenever they could afford it, they took a City Break holiday, an escapist sight-seeing and shopping combo. Over the years, they had visited Venice, Rome, New York, Edinburgh, and Paris.

This time they had come to Las Vegas for a long weekend.

Checking into their rooms at one of the big hotels on the strip (cheap as chips rates, Linda had observed when they made their booking), they headed out to see the sights and check out the shops. They would also go into the casinos but restrict themselves to a spectating role.

Sunday night saw them back in their hotel. They were due to check out early the next day.

After dinner, they went into the casino to do some more punter-watching. But this time, they decided they couldn't really go to Las Vegas and not have at least a small flutter.

So, they went their separate ways, Linda to roulette and Valerie to blackjack.

At 8:00 a.m. the next morning, they met up at the check-out desk.

Valerie gasped when she saw her bill: $4,500!

"There must be a mistake," she said.

The cashier checked the details. "Nope, it's correct, honey. You were in the casino last night and bought $3,000 worth of chips on your room account."

"But I only ordered $300 worth," exclaimed Valerie.

"I'm sorry, sweetheart. The system never gets it wrong."

Valerie turned to Linda. "What on earth am I going to do? There's no way I can pay this."

But Linda was as white as a ghost, a sheet of paper held in her trembling fingers.

"Oh no, you haven't made the same mistake, have you?"

Linda couldn't speak, couldn't even breathe.

Valerie grabbed the paper from her, and her face turned white as a sheet.

"$45,000!" she shrieked. "That's more than a year's pay. Oh, what a nightmare."

The two girls looked at each other and burst into tears, hysterical.

A security guy appeared. "You'd better come with me, ladies."

He led them into an office and left the room.

The two girls sat there, sobbing uncontrollably.

The door opened, and a smartly dressed man came in and sat down on the other side of the desk.

"I'm the Casino Manager, and it seems you two have been somewhat foolish."

There was no answer.

The man looked at the papers on his desk.

"It says here you both work as hospice nurses, so I'm guessing there's no way you're able to pay."

Again, there was no answer.

"My Mom and my Pop died in hospice care. Cancer took them both within 12 months. But they died well. The hospice nurses were terrific."

He paused and looked at the sobbing girls. Then he ripped up the papers and dropped the pieces in the waste bin.

"Have this one on us. Just don't ever be so stupid again."

• •

Jesus' eyes bore into those of the young man.

"Simon, answer me this. Who would have been the more thankful, Valerie or Linda?"

"I guess Linda, as her bill was 10 times as big."

"Exactly," said Jesus.

The parable of the debtors and creditor

Luke
7:36-50

³⁶When one of the Pharisees invited Jesus to have dinner with him, he went to the Pharisee's house and reclined at the table. ³⁷A woman in that town who lived a sinful life learned that Jesus was eating at the Pharisee's house, so she came there with an alabaster jar of perfume. ³⁸As she stood behind him at his feet weeping, she began to wet his feet with her tears. Then she wiped them with her hair, kissed them and poured perfume on them.

³⁹When the Pharisee who had invited him saw this, he said to himself, "If this man were a prophet, he would know who is touching him and what kind of woman she is—that she is a sinner."

⁴⁰Jesus answered him, "Simon, I have something to tell you."

"Tell me, teacher," he said.

⁴¹"Two people owed money to a certain moneylender. One owed him five hundred denarii, and the other fifty. ⁴²Neither of them had the money to pay him back, so he forgave the debts of both. Now which of them will love him more?"

⁴³Simon replied, "I suppose the one who had the bigger debt forgiven."

"You have judged correctly," Jesus said.

⁴⁴Then he turned toward the woman and said to Simon, "Do you see this woman? I came into your house. You did not give me any water for my feet, but she wet my feet with her tears and wiped them with her hair. ⁴⁵You did not give me a kiss, but this woman, from the time I entered, has not stopped kissing my feet. ⁴⁶You did not put oil on my head, but she has poured perfume on my feet. ⁴⁷Therefore, I tell you, her many sins have been forgiven—as her great love has shown. But whoever has been forgiven little loves little."

⁴⁸Then Jesus said to her, "Your sins are forgiven."

⁴⁹The other guests began to say among themselves, "Who is this who even forgives sins?"

⁵⁰Jesus said to the woman, "Your faith has saved you; go in peace."

So, what's this story saying to US, here and now?

We've included the whole of the original passage as we think it is important to read this parable in the context in which it was originally told. (That holds true for most of the parables, but particularly so in this case.)

Each of us frequently catches ourselves being more than somewhat self-righteous, saying something like, *"Yes, I know I need forgiveness—after all, none of us is perfect. But I haven't got too much wrong, have I? If only I was a bigger sinner, I'd be able to confess more easily."*

Sometimes we even catch ourselves thinking of someone else: They're the "real" sinners! We then tell ourselves that we may need forgiveness, but not THAT much, thank goodness. Apart from being overly judgmental (a sin), we are, of course, completely wrong. We are reminded of this every time we take communion and ask for forgiveness for the wrong things we have done in thought, word, and deed and the good things we have not done. (How long do you have, Lord?)

But even if we were as good as our deluded thoughts try to persuade us that we are, it wouldn't necessarily be an entirely good thing. Actually, we may be missing out.

A small crime requires small forgiveness; an enormous crime requires great forgiveness.

Mike's middle daughter, Felicity, was—still is—terribly accident-prone. When she was little, he learned to fear the exclamation "oops!" Generally, it would be just another glass broken, but not always. One of her greatest misdemeanors was dropping the bottle of vintage port he and his wife had saved from their wedding year to open on their silver wedding anniversary.

Of course, it had been an accident, not a thing done with purpose or intent. And her remorse, contrition, and tears were so intense that Mike couldn't do anything other than forgive. He subsequently realized that this was one of the times he loved her most.

Why should God be any different?

If we have been forgiven a lot, we know how real gratitude feels, which helps us show forgiveness and compassion to others.

The greater the forgiveness we have received, the greater our propensity and capability to fulfill our obligation to love and forgive others unconditionally.

We think that's the point this parable makes.

Reflection and prayer | Am I forgiving as I have been forgiven?

. . . .

_____

_____

_____

_____

_____

What's this story saying to me, here and now?

. . . .

_____

_____

_____

_____

_____

THE SELFISH LAWYER

With his self-centered attitude...
and his self-obsessive desires.
Will he get what he deserves?

Jesus was asked to pronounce upon a family squabble. As is so often the case, material possessions lay at the heart of it. He politely refused to become embroiled in the spat and instead told this parable:

• •

If you ever visit the UK, enter GL54 8VE into your navigator and it will take you 90 miles due west out of London along the M4, then north onto the A429 and finally—via a series of increasingly unmetalled and grass-adorned minor roads—to Little Ditching.

The trip will have been worth it, for Little Ditching is a wonderfully picturesque Cotswold village, a scene on countless greetings cards and fudge boxes.

Amazingly it has escaped the clutches of the weekend retreat market and remains home to a close-knit local community. Central to their social whirl is, of course, the local pub together with an exceptionally well-equipped village hall.

That hall has a story to tell.

It started 20 years ago when the hall was not so well equipped. To be accurate, it was in terminal decay. A structural survey had diagnosed rising dampness and sinking. The surveyor had also recommended a complete re-wiring and re-roofing, concluding with a refurbishment estimate of over $300,000—well beyond the means of the village community. The hall had no architectural or historical provenance, so no grants would be forthcoming. Even though it was home to the local Girl Scouts, Boy Scouts, an amateur dramatic theatre company, and numerous other societies, it contravened just about every Health and Safety regulation. So, the village steeled itself for its inevitable closure and probable demolition.

One of the more recent residents was a 50-year-old commercial lawyer who had used a year-end bonus and an unexpected bequest from a distant relative to

fund his early retirement. Soon after his arrival in the village he had a second stroke of good fortune. This time it was truly a fortune: a $24 million lottery win.

Having not bothered to tick the "no publicity" box, he was soon overcome with approaches from any number of good causes. He did not in any way find this a problem, having decided from the outset that good causes didn't come any better than himself!

A long-time admirer of modern art, he was soon a familiar figure in Mayfair's best galleries and auction houses. Fascination turned to obsession. He converted his basement into a private display area. Obsession turned to perversion. This was his collection: for his eyes only. Every night he would retreat to his gallery, pour himself a large Scotch—or several—and suffuse himself in self-content.

When the Health and Safety officials forced the immediate closure of the village hall, he unexpectedly contacted the Town Clerk with an offer of help. Great rejoicing all round quickly soured when it became apparent that his idea of help was to acquire the hall (at a knock-down price) and convert it into a private gallery (for his use only) for his art collection, which by now had outgrown his basement. The council, realizing they had no other options, reluctantly accepted his offer.

A no-expense-spared makeover saw the hall immaculately restored. The roof was renewed. Foundations underpinned, a mezzanine floor added, and air-conditioning was installed throughout.

The art collection was transferred, more pieces were acquired, and a set of six sculptures was specially commissioned for the reopening ceremony, an opening to which a grand total of one person was invited: himself. After all, this was a private gallery. The public could go whistle.

The day before the opening, he could hardly contain himself. As the day wore on, his nervous excitement triggered a migraine. Determined not to let this spoil the occasion, he retired to bed with aspirin and a very large Scotch.

Two months later, the Parish Council reacquired the hall for the same price they had sold it.

The art collection was in the hands of a leading auctioneer.

And the commercial lawyer was in a nursing home.

The stroke he suffered that night had spared his life but left him paralyzed—and blind.

The parable of the rich fool

Luke
12:13-21

¹³Someone in the crowd said to him, "Teacher, tell my brother to divide the inheritance with me."

¹⁴Jesus replied, "Man, who appointed me a judge or an arbiter between you?" ¹⁵Then he said to them, "Watch out! Be on your guard against all kinds of greed; life does not consist in an abundance of possessions."

¹⁶And he told them this parable: "The ground of a certain rich man yielded an abundant harvest. ¹⁷He thought to himself, 'What shall I do? I have no place to store my crops.'

¹⁸"Then he said, 'This is what I'll do. I will tear down my barns and build bigger ones, and there I will store my surplus grain. ¹⁹And I'll say to myself, "You have plenty of grain laid up for many years. Take life easy; eat, drink and be merry."'

²⁰"But God said to him, 'You fool! This very night your life will be demanded from you. Then who will get what you have prepared for yourself?'

²¹"This is how it will be with whoever stores up things for themselves but is not rich toward God."

So, what's this story saying to US, here and now?

A dramatic tale. Chilling even. And certainly tragic.

But, like all the parables, it's told to drive home a simple message.

In this case: live life generously.

God longs to bless our lives.

Sometimes we may feel (wrongly) that we have earned that blessing.

At other times, it just seems to drop into our laps.

Most of us will have experienced both types of blessing on our lives.

The commercial lawyer had clearly worked hard at his job, sufficiently so to achieve success and a bumper bonus by the age of 50. Rewards well-earned. On the other hand, the lottery win was completely fortuitous.

The rich farmer in the original parable would have worked hard to make his money too. The bumper harvest was unexpected icing on the cake.

Either way, both were richly blessed.

Jesus is not saying that you should not enjoy your blessings.

But he is saying that how you enjoy them is important. If someone does us a great favor, our natural instinct is to look to pay them back somehow.

But God doesn't want us to pay his blessings back. He wants us to pay them forward.

Blessings are not given to us solely for our own benefit. We should always look to share our blessings: to use them to bless other people.

There's also a very important sub-plot in this parable regarding our attitude to our possessions. Are they serving us or are we serving them? Are they just objects or have they become objects of worship? If, for any reason, God were to ask us, would we be prepared to let them go?

Reflection and prayer | Am I living my life generously?

What's this story saying to **me,** here and now?

THE STORY OF THE NIGHT WATCH

Always on guard...against being off-guard. Were they caught napping?

Jesus told this story to stress to his disciples the importance of them maintaining their spiritual alertness:

· ·

Faces glowed ghostly white in the darkness as light snow drifted down.

B Platoon was on a night exercise in North Slope, Alaska.

Their mission: to hold a gun emplacement against a suspected enemy attack.

Lieutenant Garcia was in charge. Her Captain had been summoned to a staff meeting at HQ an hour ago.

Watch-keeping was being done in pairs, each stretch just an hour long to maintain maximum alertness.

The snow became heavier, and it lay like a winter duvet, muffling and deadening sound. The hours passed.

Suddenly a noise. In reality, a snow-laden twig snapped, but it broke the eerie silence like a pistol shot.

"Gee, thanks, Cap. It really challenges your attention doesn't it, not knowing when things are going to happen?"

"Too right, son," replied his Captain.

"You can never afford to let your guard down, no matter who you are. In 1944, if Rommel had anticipated the invasion, our boys would never have got off the beaches.

"Always expect the unexpected. That's my motto."

The sentry whipped around and levelled his rifle: "Halt and identify yourself!"

"Willis Tower" came the reply, the passcode for that night.

"Advance."

The figure of Captain Caffrey emerged from the snow.

"Well done, son. It's nearly dawn. You can stand down. Give me your rifle, and I'll take the next shift."

The parable of the alert servants

Luke
12:35-40

³⁵"Be dressed ready for service and keep your lamps burning, ³⁶like servants waiting for their master to return from a wedding banquet, so that when he comes and knocks they can immediately open the door for him. ³⁷It will be good for those servants whose master finds them watching when he comes. Truly I tell you, he will dress himself to serve, will have them recline at the table and will come and wait on them. ³⁸It will be good for those servants whose master finds them ready, even if he comes in the middle of the night or toward daybreak. ³⁹But understand this: If the owner of the house had known at what hour the thief was coming, he would not have let his house be broken into. ⁴⁰You also must be ready, because the Son of Man will come at an hour when you do not expect him."

So, what's this story saying to US, here and now?

"Always expect the unexpected" was Captain Caffrey's motto.

Not unexpectedly, it's the sort of thing you'd expect to hear from a soldier.

Unexpected things, good and bad, happen to us pretty frequently: a twenty-dollar lottery win, a tire blowout, a surprise call from a friend, or a power outage.

Life is full of surprises, unexpected things that we are not expecting.

But what unexpected news and occurrences should we be expecting?

How about prophecies? And miracles?

Nah, they don't happen now do they?

Are we sure? When was the last time you heard a word from God?

Have you ever heard one?

If you have, the chances are it was while reading the Bible, during a service, in conversation with a Christian friend, or in a time of prayer and contemplation.

Chances are that the same applies to the last time God intervened in your life to remove or ease a problem or create an opportunity.

Prophecies and miracles are unexpected occurrences. They don't come to order.

But we should nevertheless expect them to happen, and we can express that expectation through consistent, purposeful, anticipatory prayer.

God's word to us and his hand on our life tend to come unexpectedly.

But that doesn't mean we shouldn't expect it.

"Always expect the unexpected."

Reflection and prayer | How great are my expectations?

. . . .

What's this story saying to **me,** here and now?

. . . .

THE TALE OF THE CEO'S DILEMMA

Who to back...and who to sack?
Who was found lacking?

When Jesus had finished telling the story of the Alert Servants (see: *Night Watch*), Peter was keen to know whether it was meant for them, the disciples, or for everyone. Typically, Jesus' response took the form of another story:

• •

Ebony Williams was in a quandary.

As CEO of Time and Space Enterprises, she was responsible for delivering the 3-year Strategic Plan and the Annual Operating Profits.

That wasn't her quandary. She could do that falling off a log backward and had done for the past seven years (delivered the results, that is, not fallen off a log).

But it is a truism that you can be a victim of your own success. And boy, was that the case now.

The Board of TSE had been approached by a large publishing company struggling to shift from print to streaming, from analog to digital.

Under Ebony's guidance, TSE had managed to do just that, with considerable success. Now the media publishing company wanted to shelter under the same umbrella. Their shareholders had voted to merge with TSE, providing Ebony took the CEO role for the combined companies.

The TSE Board had bitten off the proffered, dollar-filled hand.

Now Ebony had to relocate from TSE's base in Kansas City to New York.

But that wasn't her quandary, either. She'd worked for two years in NYC earlier in her career and had no problem with returning. Quite the reverse. She loved the city.

No, her quandary was what to do with the management team at TSE in Kansas.

Ebony had two lieutenants.

Ernie Mountjoy ran the organization's print assets, magazines, and newspapers that had successfully managed the analog-to-digital transition and still delivered a reasonable, but declining, part of the group's profit. Instinctively protective of his people and reluctant to make fast decisions, Ernie Mountjoy had been rechristened "Erm."

Then there was Mitch Miller, the boss of the rapidly growing broadcast and video division. Never one to shy away from a difficult decision, he was commonly known as "Rich Killer." He liked to take the fast, relentless, and ruthless route to success.

With Ebony in day-to-day control, it had all worked out just fine. The two represented a perfect cocktail of management. But now that Ebony was off to NYC, the cherry was leaving the glass.

She feared that, in her absence, the two would live up to their nicknames: Erm would be overly protective of his declining republic, and Rich Killer would be overly ruthless in building his expanding empire.

But it was far, far worse than that.

Twelve months later, Ebony extricated herself from the demands of the now hugely successful NYC business and spent a week in Kansas assessing the TSE business there, reviewing performance and scrutinizing their plans for the year ahead.

She was both pleasantly surprised and totally horrified by what she found.

Pleasantly surprised because Erm's division had managed to grow its revenues and profits, not hugely, but it far exceeded her expectations of a rapid decline. She decided that Erm had proved his worth and would get a step up in the enlarged organization.

But totally horrified when she saw that Killer's division, of which she had expected much, had totally imploded. Revenues were down by 30%, and profits were all but eradicated.

On closer examination, it became clear that Mitch had been drinking his own Kool-Aid.

Long lunches and dinners with his cronies had overridden his judgment and alienated his producers and writers. Most of the creative talent had deserted to work for other broadcasters. Advertising monies followed them. Unusually for an industry characterized by "Minnesota Nice," several long-serving and well-respected industry veterans told Ebony exactly why they detested Mitch. Frequent descriptors were that he was arrogant, drunk, overbearing, calculatedly ruthless, and insensitive.

Interestingly, no one accused him of being stupid. He was more than capable of running the business successfully, but had lost the plot, led astray by his self-indulgence and undone by his anti-social demeanor.

Ebony knew she needed to have a difficult conversation with Mitch.

"Mitch, you're fired with immediate effect. Clear your desk and go now. You knew what I wanted you to do. If I thought there was any doubt about that, I would be more lenient. But you knew it, and you ignored it. As a result, other people suffered. Tell me if I'm wrong."

Mitch left. Not because he knew so little and did too much, but because he knew so much and yet did too little.

The parable of the faithful steward

Luke
12:41-48

⁴¹Peter asked, "Lord, are you telling this parable to us, or to everyone?"

⁴²The Lord answered, "Who then is the faithful and wise manager, whom the master puts in charge of his servants to give them their food allowance at the proper time? ⁴³It will be good for that servant whom the master finds doing so when he returns. ⁴⁴Truly I tell you, he will put him in charge of all his possessions. ⁴⁵But suppose the servant says to himself, 'My master is taking a long time in coming,' and he then begins to beat the other servants, both men and women, and to eat and drink and get drunk. ⁴⁶The master of that servant will come on a day when he does not expect him and at an hour he is not aware of. He will cut him to pieces and assign him a place with the unbelievers.

⁴⁷"The servant who knows the master's will and does not get ready or does not do what the master wants will be beaten with many blows. ⁴⁸But the one who does not know and does things deserving punishment will be beaten with few blows. From everyone who has been given much, much will be demanded; and from the one who has been entrusted with much, much more will be asked."

So, what's this story saying to US, here and now?

This parable packs a real punch. Here it is in Jesus' own words:

"From everyone who has been given much, much will be demanded; and from the one who has been entrusted with much, much more will be asked" (Luke 12:48).

Ivan is a business professor. At one university, two professorial colleagues met with him every morning for coffee and conversation.

One morning, when Ivan was preparing to teach a class on business ethics, one of the professors asked him, "What do you consider the most unethical practice in most organizations?"

Ivan thought about it.

"Do you mean stealing? If you do, I don't think it's stealing pencils and envelopes."

"Yes, it is a form of stealing, but, no, not pencils or envelopes."

"I give up. What is it?"

"It's people not using their talents to their fullest extent. That's stealing from the organization and, worse still, cheating on God."

Making the most of our God-given talents, giving our best shot, is part of our worship of God. Blessing as we have been blessed.

Ernie, the low flyer, by making the most of his limited talents, made a positive contribution.

Mitch, the high flyer, by not using his talents well, was in effect stealing.

It's all too easy for us to coast along at work or church, in our homes or social networks, and not always bring our A-Game.

But here's the thing: Jesus is not a fan of second best.

Good enough, just isn't.

So, to repeat Peter's question: is the story being told to us or everyone?

What do we think?

Reflection and prayer | Am I bringing my A-game?

· ·

_____

_____

_____

_____

_____

What's this story saying to **me,** here and now?

· ·

_____

_____

_____

_____

_____

THE FAILING PROJECT

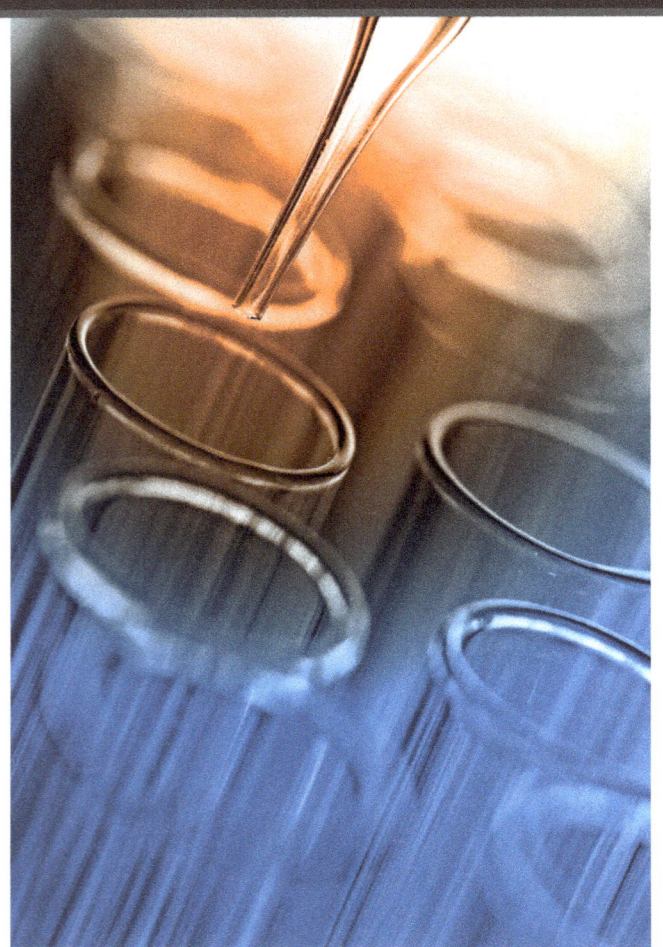

Three years of work...with nothing to show. Time to pull the plug?

All of us can be tempted to put off doing something difficult.

Like saying sorry to someone.

Even to God.

Jesus urged his disciples not to procrastinate:

· ·

"Sorry, but I think it's time we pulled the plug on this one."

The Chief Executive of the American Medical Research Institute was visiting their Research & Development Center in Houston.

"We've been working flat out on this vaccine for three years now and have gotten absolutely nowhere. We're wasting valuable resources that could be better used elsewhere, so I'm going to shut the project down."

The project head, Dr Lyn Cooper, quickly interceded. "Sir, I understand your frustration, but it's a vital project, and I think we should push on, one more time. I'll reshuffle the team and pull in some new faces.

"If we've still nothing to show this time next year, then by all means, close the project down."

The parable of the fig tree without figs

Luke
13:1-9

¹Now there were some present at that time who told Jesus about the Galileans whose blood Pilate had mixed with their sacrifices. ²Jesus answered, "Do you think that these Galileans were worse sinners than all the other Galileans because they suffered this way? ³I tell you, no! But unless you repent, you too will all perish. ⁴Or those eighteen who died when the tower in Siloam fell on them—do you think they were more guilty than all the others living in Jerusalem? ⁵I tell you, no! But unless you repent, you too will all perish."

⁶Then he told this parable: "A man had a fig tree growing in his vineyard, and he went to look for fruit on it but did not find any. ⁷So he said to the man who took care of the vineyard, 'For three years now I've been coming to look for fruit on this fig tree and haven't found any. Cut it down! Why should it use up the soil?'

⁸"'Sir,' the man replied, 'leave it alone for one more year, and I'll dig around it and fertilize it. ⁹If it bears fruit next year, fine! If not, then cut it down.'"

So, what's this story saying to US, here and now?

Jesus' ministry lasted for three years. The fig tree had been growing without fruit for three years.

A coincidence?

We think not.

Jesus was too purposeful a storyteller for that. We're sure he used the three years deliberately.

So, we've kept the same timescale in our rewiring.

Let's look at the context of the parable.

In Jesus' day, people were concerned about human rights atrocities and natural disasters. A repressive regime; a catastrophic accident. Not unlike the news bulletins of today.

But, in those days, they weren't seen as accidents. They were regarded as acts of God, punishments: "Boy, those people must have been really bad. Lucky for us, we're not as bad as they are."

"No, no, no," says Jesus. "You've got it all wrong. Those people were no better or worse than you. Unless you repent of your sins, truly repent of them, then in God's eyes, you're as bad as anyone else."

This would have been truly shocking stuff for his audience.

Then, Jesus drives it home, saying, in effect: "Look, despite all my teaching and preaching, you're still not getting the message. Get your act together before it's too late."

But he sweetens the pill. The fig tree is given another year. Did it eventually produce figs? Did the scientists create the vaccine?

Typically, a fig tree will not produce fruit until it is at least two years old. It can take up to six years. Big research projects too do not provide instant results.

We're not told what happened. But that is not the point.

The point is that the extra time was given.

In our case, time to say sorry.

Cleverly, the parable does not let this stay of execution detract from the message's urgency. Jesus will always give us more time, but anyone without Jesus in his or her life needs to bear in mind that, in this physical life, time is not infinite.

Footnote: *After writing this last paragraph, we were struck by another thought. Many of us may be praying for a family member or a friend to discover Jesus. We may have been praying for years. And we should continue to pray because Jesus doesn't really mind how long it takes someone to come to him, just as long as they do. And when they do, it's PARTY time!*

Reflection and prayer | Is time on my side?

· ·

_____

_____

_____

_____

_____

What's this story saying to **me,** here and now?

· ·

_____

_____

_____

_____

_____

THE RELUCTANT ADVERTISER

Persuaded to go big...and splash the cash. Does risk bring reward?

Jesus has been through a busy few days of traveling, teaching, healing people, and clashing with the Pharisees. He tries to grab a bit of me-time on a lake shore, but the crowds continued to build, and they find him. So, Jesus climbs into a boat, rows a short way off the shore, and uses it as a platform to tell one of his most famous parables:

• •

Emma Rossi astounded her parents by painting her first watercolor landscape when she was just three years old. Twenty-two years later, she had added seascapes to her repertoire and oils to her palette. Her portfolio was as extensive as her holiday travels, which covered four continents.

A friend persuaded her to turn her hobby into a business, so she rented a small shop in Des Moines and opened an art gallery.

At the end of her first week, just two people had come inside, one to ask directions to City Hall, the other thinking it was a new coffee shop.

That weekend she sought out her friend. "Well, I've gone for it as you advised, but I think it may have been a big mistake."

"You should advertise the gallery," came the suggestion.

"Don't be crazy," Emma replied. "Everyone knows that's just a waste of money because it's expensive and people ignore ads these days. So, I'm using social media."

Her friend sucked her teeth. "Hmm, social media? I'm not convinced that's going to work. You need to reach out way beyond your own social network. Yes, it's true that if you put an ad in the paper, some people will not even notice it. Others will see it but ignore it. Still, others will see it, and be interested. but then turn the page and forget it as something else grabs their attention. But there will also be those who will see it, be interested in it, remember it, and come visit your gallery. And they will give you a huge return on your investment. Trust me on this."

So Emma emptied her bank account and bought a full-color, double-page spread in the Des Moines Register. Within two weeks, she had sold three-quarters of her stock and received dozens of new commissions.

The parable of the sower

Matthew
13:1-9

¹*That same day Jesus went out of the house and sat by the lake. ²Such large crowds gathered around him that he got into a boat and sat in it, while all the people stood on the shore. ³Then he told them many things in parables, saying: "A farmer went out to sow his seed. ⁴As he was scattering the seed, some fell along the path, and the birds came and ate it up. ⁵Some fell on rocky places, where it did not have much soil. It sprang up quickly, because the soil was shallow. ⁶But when the sun came up, the plants were scorched, and they withered because they had no root. ⁷Other seed fell among thorns, which grew up and choked the plants. ⁸Still other seed fell on good soil, where it produced a crop—a hundred, sixty or thirty times what was sown. ⁹Whoever has ears, let them hear."*

**Luke
8:4-8**

**Mark
4:1-9**

⁴While a large crowd was gathering and people were coming to Jesus from town after town, he told this parable: ⁵"A farmer went out to sow his seed. As he was scattering the seed, some fell along the path; it was trampled on, and the birds ate it up. ⁶Some fell on rocky ground, and when it came up, the plants withered because they had no moisture. ⁷Other seed fell among thorns, which grew up with it and choked the plants. ⁸Still other seed fell on good soil. It came up and yielded a crop, a hundred times more than was sown."

When he said this, he called out, "Whoever has ears to hear, let them hear."

¹Again Jesus began to teach by the lake. The crowd that gathered around him was so large that he got into a boat and sat in it out on the lake, while all the people were along the shore at the water's edge. ²He taught them many things by parables, and in his teaching said: ³"Listen! A farmer went out to sow his seed.

⁴As he was scattering the seed, some fell along the path, and the birds came and ate it up. ⁵Some fell on rocky places, where it did not have much soil. It sprang up quickly, because the soil was shallow. ⁶But when the sun came up, the plants were scorched, and they withered because they had no root. ⁷Other seed fell among thorns, which grew up and choked the plants, so that they did not bear grain. ⁸Still other seed fell on good soil. It came up, grew and produced a crop, some multiplying thirty, some sixty, some a hundred times."

⁹Then Jesus said, "Whoever has ears to hear, let them hear."

So, what's this story saying to US, here and now?

We love this parable! It's about the three S's: the Sower, the Seed, and the Soil.

Most of the sermons we have heard preached on this parable have focused on the seed and the soil, God's word, the hearers of that word, and the contrasting outcomes. Indeed, this is what Jesus focused on when he explained the parable to his disciples.

But Mike's an adman, and when he came to preach on it, he decided to look at the Sower. Here's what he said:

At first glance he seems a pretty careless chap, doesn't he? Seed was a precious commodity in those days, almost a currency. A good yield is critical to a good harvest, and a good harvest critical to life. The key to this was good seed, carefully sown into well-prepared and cultivated ground. And yet here's this guy chucking it all over the place!

Why? And who is this fellow?

In the parable, the seed is the message about the kingdom. The Sower can be anyone who is spreading the word. But, at the time of the parable, the man doing the most spreading was Jesus. So, let's consider this an autobiographical parable with Jesus in the lead role.

Was he being careless and irresponsible, wasting precious seed by preaching to all and sundry (even Samaritans and lepers)?

Or was he being lavishly and lovingly extravagant? Making sure that everyone had the opportunity to hear about and to receive God's grace?

I know what I think. How about you?

The other reason I love this parable is that I learned my advertising trade during the golden years of advertising in the 70s and 80s. Building big brands during the days of mass-audience TV and mass-market broadcast print media.

We didn't worry too much about Google analytics-style precision targeting then. We just ran interesting and entertaining ads conveying a strong brand message to a mass audience and waited for people to react. Of course, not everyone became a buyer, but the return on investment from those that did was huge. And even if people didn't buy the product, they still talked about the ad which helped fuel word of mouth.

There's a clear message here to the church today, and to anyone who wants to help get the word out: be extravagant. Take a risk.

Let's not be too hung-up about getting God's word out to exactly the "right" people at just the right time in precisely the right way. Let's be like the Sower and just throw it out there, big time!"

Reflection and prayer | Am I throwing it out, big time?

· ·

_____

_____

_____

_____

_____

What's this story saying to me, here and now?

· ·

_____

_____

_____

_____

LISTEN UP!

(THE SHOW'S ABOUT TO START)

Congratulations! You've reached the end of the first leg of your road trip with Jesus.

He's been touring around towns and villages, recruiting disciples, attracting followers, and building a reputation that is spreading far and wide.

All without recourse to social media.

(Good old word of mouth. Never underestimate it.)

He's announced himself and his mission in the parables of new cloth and new wine.

In the parable of the lamp under the bushel he's put himself in the spotlight.

He's then gone on to teach about wisdom, faith, forgiveness, generosity, expectant prayer, equality, justice, and inclusivity.

Like a good adman, he's caught your attention and whetted your appetite to hear more stories.

And like a good adman, he knows he now has to get to his 'pitch'.

And that means he has to start focusing on the promise that lies at the heart of his teaching campaign: the Kingdom of God: what it is like and why it matters.

But that would prove to be no easy matter…

COMING SOON
'HEAVEN IS...'
'The ultimate feel-good factor'
'A 5-star blockbuster'
★★★★★

Have you ever tried to explain to someone what Heaven is like? If so, you've probably discovered that it's not as easy as it might seem.

But don't worry, you're in good company.

Jesus wanted his people to know the secrets of the Kingdom of God. These are not secrets hidden in some secret society initiation ceremony, but secrets hidden in plain sight, obvious to those who have eyes to see and ears to hear.

He tells the following series of stories to illustrate that.

![JUNK MAIL](image of a hand holding a phone displaying an email inbox screen)

1:29

Email

< Mailboxes   Edit

... 🔍

● **Political Fallout**
New Polls are Shocking!
Click to see the latest polls that confirm...

● **Green Energy**
Study Shows Significant Enviromental Impact
Scientists in the UK have published a study...

● **Tech Solutions**
Upgrade Your Devices Now
The latest round of upgrades have made a...

● **Ultimate Fitness**
Achieve your fitness goals!
No cost access; start transforming now...

● **Sports Authority**
The Champs are Back
Defending their big win last year, the North...

● **Home Comfort**
Cozy living starts here!
Browse our collection, comfort awaits...

● **Luxury Homes**
Own a dream home today!
Explore our listings now, dream big...

● **Economic Prospector**
Inflation is moving in the right direction.

Inbox   Flagged   Draft   Trash   Send

The killer filter...that may be too lethal.
Will the good get wasted with the bad?

Anusha Kapur closed the folder and placed it on the desk. With her chin resting upon steepled fingers she looked intently at the man sitting opposite her.

"How long have you worked for the Orlando Sentinel, Rob?"

"Just over five years."

"And always in IT?"

"Yep."

"Hmmm. Well, I've only been here as the editor for three months. Clearly, I don't know our systems as well as you. But I've been a journalist for 12 years and what I can tell you is that this proposal to install a high-grade email filter is completely unacceptable."

Rob bristled and leaned forward in his chair.

"Why on earth not, Anusha? I've studied our working practices, and I can tell you that having this new filter will reduce the average inbox size by 60% and mas-

sively increase productivity. Do you realize how much time our journalists spend sifting through their emails? The return on investment will be huge."

"It's not a matter of cost, Rob. Look, the reason that journalists spend so much time plowing through emails is that they're looking for stories. Good stories. The trouble is that they take some digging out because they are not always obvious. Many of them come from quite dubious sources, so an aggressive junk mail filter would have a heyday. I'm sure you are right that inbox sizes would drop by 60%, maybe even more. But I'm equally sure we'd lose more than 60% of our stories.

"I'm sorry, Rob, but our journalists are going to have to carry on doing what they've always done. Open their inboxes, work their way through all their emails, root out the good stories, and only then hit the delete button on the remainder."

Once Rob had left the office, Anusha picked up the folder and gently slid it into her waste bin.

The parable of the weeds

Matthew 13:24-30

²⁴Jesus told them another parable: "The kingdom of heaven is like a man who sowed good seed in his field. ²⁵But while everyone was sleeping, his enemy came and sowed weeds among the wheat, and went away. ²⁶When the wheat sprouted and formed heads, then the weeds also appeared.

²⁷"The owner's servants came to him and said, 'Sir, didn't you sow good seed in your field? Where then did the weeds come from?'

²⁸"'An enemy did this,' he replied.

"The servants asked him, 'Do you want us to go and pull them up?'

²⁹"'No,' he answered, 'because while you are pulling the weeds, you may uproot the wheat with them. ³⁰Let both grow together until the harvest. At that time, I will tell the harvesters: First collect the weeds and tie them in bundles to be burned; then gather the wheat and bring it into my barn.'"

So, what's this story saying to US, here and now?

This parable follows hard on the heels of the Sower.

That parable focused on the diligent farmer (Jesus) sowing good seed. This one focuses on his sworn enemy (Satan) sowing bad seed.

In warfare, disinformation and disruption are key strategies.

Propaganda is used to undermine morale and fifth columnists are deployed to undermine (literally) communications and infrastructure.

A "false flag" procedure saw Russia put "peacekeeping" tanks into Ukraine.

From the very beginning of the story of humanity, Satan has been the prince of such deceit, the arch-proponent of half-truths. In the Garden of Eden, he said to Eve:

"Did God really say?" ... "You will not surely die."

Jesus experienced these weapons personally in his confrontation with the devil in the wilderness, facing half-truths and distortions:

"If you are the Son of God?" ... "For it is written."

Make no mistake, these are powerful tactics.

As the saying goes:

"A lie can sprint halfway around the world before truth has put its sneakers on."

As we pursue our mission to build the Kingdom of God on earth as it is in Heaven, we need to beware of Satan sowing the weeds of discontent.

Reflection and prayer | Is Satan sowing weeds in my life?

· ·

_____

_____

_____

_____

_____

What's this story saying to **me,** here and now?

· ·

_____

_____

_____

_____

_____

THE RETIREMENT FUND

Polly receives a large legacy...should she enjoy it or invest it? Spend or save?

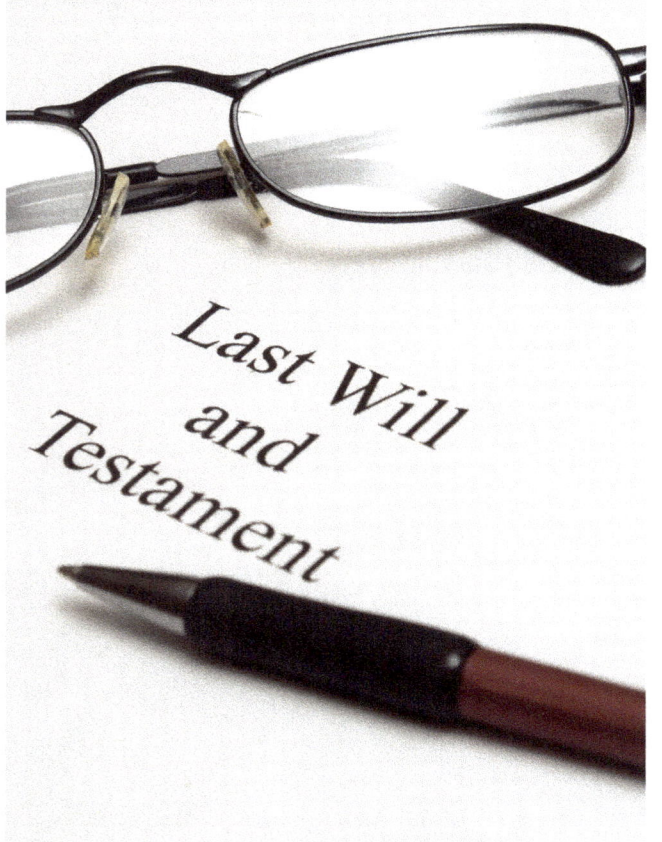

Last Will and Testament

Polly was by no means rich. In fact, as a single parent (her husband having run off with another woman shortly after the birth of their son) she often found it hard to make ends meet.

But somehow, she got by. Life in a rental in a trailer park in Omaha, Nebraska, wasn't so bad. It was actually a pretty good community for her toddler son to grow up in. It was safe. And there were plenty of folks living far worse lives.

When Jack was five, he started elementary school, and Polly was able to resume her job as a teacher at the same school, which was convenient. The pay wasn't huge, but at least it paid the bills.

Then one day, she received an unexpected windfall—a large bequest from her great aunt. What to do? Take Jack to Disneyland? Buy a new car? Buy a house?

All were attractive options, but Polly took some time to think ahead and instead invested the money into a retirement fund.

Then she got on with her life.

While she did her job (rising to become school principal) the fund managers got on with theirs, and the fund grew.

Thirty years later, she was ready to retire. By this time, Jack had graduated from College, pursued a lucrative career on Wall Street, married, and had two kids of his own.

Polly's investments had grown considerably, such that her retirement was better than her wildest hopes, so much so that she was able to take a tax-free sum, buy a new car, and take Jack, his wife, and her grandchildren to Disneyland.

She decided to continue to live in the trailer park, where folks were good, and she felt safe. But she did upgrade from her aging singlewide rental to become the proud owner of a brand new triplewide that could accommodate all of Jack's family when they came to visit.

Life was perfect.

The parable of the growing seed

Mark
4:26-29

²⁶He also said, "This is what the kingdom of God is like. A man scatters seed on the ground. ²⁷Night and day, whether he sleeps or gets up, the seed sprouts and grows, though he does not know how. ²⁸All by itself the soil produces grain—first the stalk, then the head, then the full kernel in the head. ²⁹As soon as the grain is ripe, he puts the sickle to it, because the harvest has come."

So, what's this story saying to  US, here and now?

Some of Jesus' parables are firecrackers. Others, on the surface, can seem pretty mundane.

This one falls in the latter category:

Dude plants seed. Seed grows. Dude harvests.

The agricultural process that has been going on since Noah was a nipper.

But we need to dig below the surface.

Jesus was keen to point out that God's kingdom has its roots, its origins, in the way we live out our life of faith.

Jesus used the analogy of someone planting seeds to grow a crop. We've rewired it as a retirement fund growing from Polly's initial payment.

Neither the seed-sower nor Polly knew for certain what the return would be on the planting and investment. Neither quite understood how it would all happen. The process was beyond their control.

In both cases it was an act of faith.

The bumper harvest, the big fund pay-out was the result of that act of faith. All the seed-sowing man and Polly had to do was live their lives faithfully, trusting in the outcome.

An act of faith is also the key to reaching God's kingdom.

Once we have committed ourselves to Jesus, we should get on and live out our lives of faith, faithfully and joyfully, trusting and secure, in the knowledge that somehow, somewhere, completely beyond our control, God is preparing an eternal bumper harvest for us.

Reflection and prayer | What might my 'final dividend' look like?

. . . .

_____

_____

_____

_____

_____

What's this story saying to me, here and now?

. . . .

_____

_____

_____

_____

_____

LOOK UP
AND LOOK IN

A concrete mix poured in New Orleans...
a cup of water poured into the Pacific.
End of...or start of?

If you want a picture of Heaven, think of it as a landmark building like Caesars Superdome, the home of the New Orleans Saints. It started off as a single concrete pour but grew into a structure that seats huge, vibrant, passionate crowds enjoying a spectacular, shared experience.

Imagine the Etihad Towers in Abu Dhabi, UAE, where the initial foundations now support five massive towers that are home to many residents and businesses, a shopping mall, 11 restaurants, and a 5-star hotel.

Or consider the massive theme park industry in Florida that was kicked off by the Magic Kingdom, but which grew so much that the Sunshine State is also now the *Funshine State.*

Think too of *The Star-Spangled Banner* being sung at the Super Bowl, which may start as a lone voice (albeit a very famous one) but grows and swells as people join in, until it encompasses the whole stadium.

Imagine a "wave" started by a small group at Fenway Park, but which eventually has more than 35,000 people participating.

Or a cup of water poured into the Pacific Ocean, the molecules of which spread globally, to the extent that some of them will be present in another cup of water taken from the Atlantic just months later.

The parable of the mustard seed and the yeast

Matthew 13:31-33

Mark 4:30-32

Luke 13:18-21

[31]He told them another parable: "The kingdom of heaven is like a mustard seed, which a man took and planted in his field. [32]Though it is the smallest of all seeds, yet when it grows, it is the largest of garden plants and becomes a tree, so that the birds come and perch in its branches."

[33]He told them still another parable: "The kingdom of heaven is like yeast that a woman took and mixed into about sixty pounds of flour until it worked all through the dough."

[30]Again he said, "What shall we say the kingdom of God is like, or what parable shall we use to describe it? [31]It is like a mustard seed, which is the smallest of all seeds on earth. [32]Yet when planted, it grows and becomes the largest of all garden plants, with such big branches that the birds can perch in its shade."

[18]Then Jesus asked, "What is the kingdom of God like? What shall I compare it to? [19]It is like a mustard seed, which a man took and planted in his garden. It grew and became a tree, and the birds perched in its branches."

[20]Again he asked, "What shall I compare the kingdom of God to? [21]It is like yeast that a woman took and mixed into about sixty pounds of flour until it worked all through the dough."

So, what's this story saying to US, here and now?

Jesus is seeking to give some tangibility to an otherwise fairly abstract concept.

A mustard seed and yeast are living organisms.

We've tried to extend that into a greater sense of physicality in our rewiring, adding a sense of community and participation.

Many people will see Heaven as an ethereal, intangible place of angels, harps, and clouds.

No, says Jesus. It's as real, more real, than all the places you have ever visited or experiences you have ever shared and enjoyed on Earth.

As real as Caesars Superdome and the Etihad Towers, Fenway Park, and the Pacific Ocean.

Heaven is all these and more.

Getting back to the mustard seed and yeast, the other point about living organisms is that they grow and expand.

In that respect, Heaven has no maximum capacity. So, let's make sure it includes us.

Especially as Jesus has already paid our price of admission.

Reflection and prayer | Do I have my ticket to the Heavenly Kingdom?

．．

_____

_____

_____

_____

_____

What's this story saying to me, here and now?

．．

_____

_____

_____

_____

_____

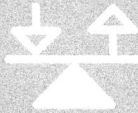

THE NICKEL
AND THE CARP

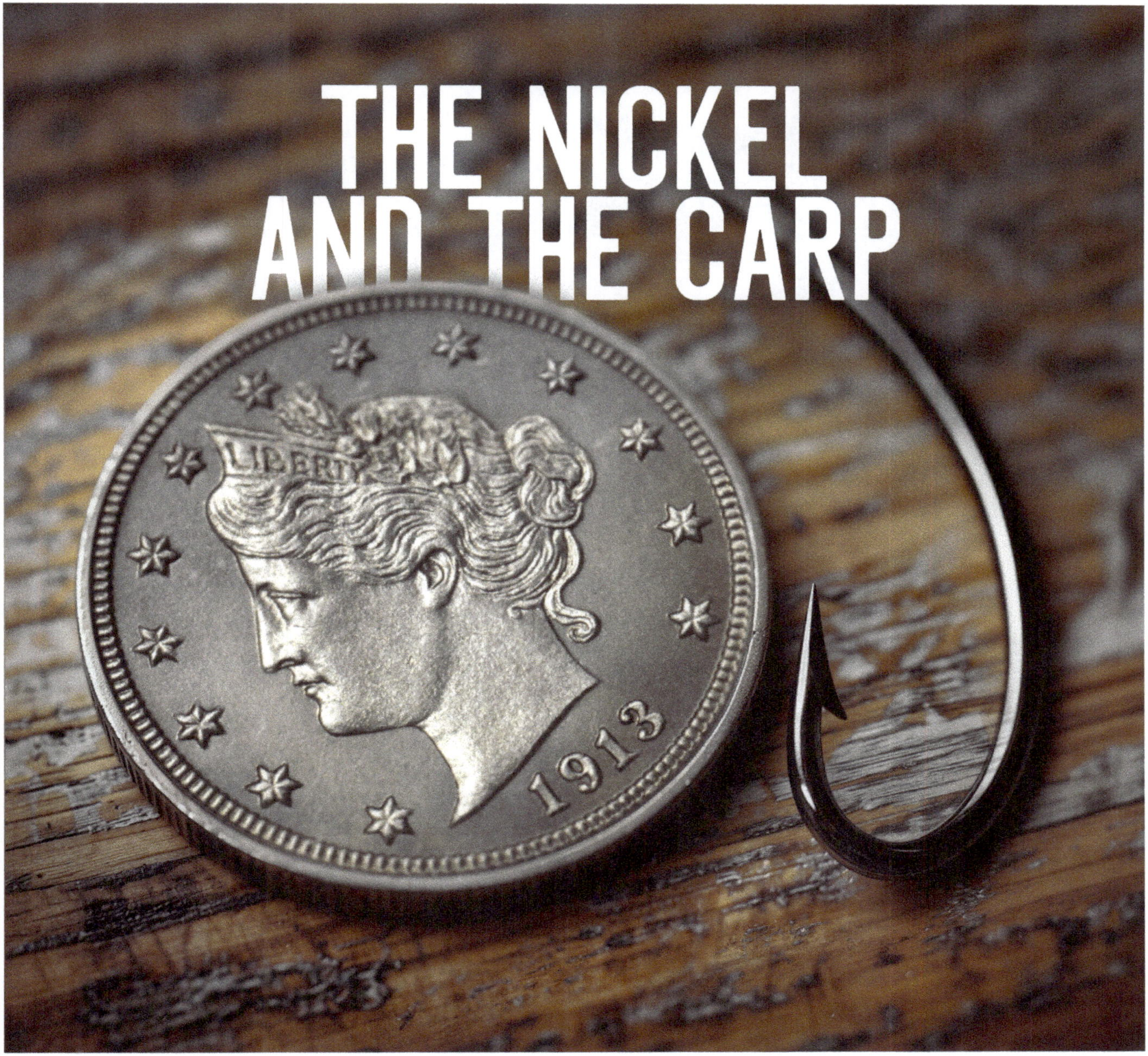

High-end specimens...with a price tag to match. Are they worth it?

The Lincoln head swam into view and grew larger as the magnifying glass hovered over it.

Above Lincoln's head were the words 'In God we trust'. To the left, the word 'Liberty'. To the right, the date: 1943 with a 'D' beneath. The back revealed the distinctive wheat laurel. All pretty regular. A 1943 Lincoln wheat cent. A copper coin, minted in Denver.

Hang on a moment though. All pennies minted in 1943 were made of steel, not copper.

Except for one. But maybe it was not alone.

Could this be an exceedingly rare, 1943-D Lincoln head *copper* penny?

Dennis Rowland's life had taken a distinct downturn in recent years. First, his electrical wholesale business in Williamsport, Pennsylvania, had failed. Shortly after, his wife walked off with one of his best friends. Hard on the heels of that, he suffered a pulmonary embolism that left him hospitalized with a collapsed lung. To cap it all, while he was recuperating, the bank foreclosed on his mortgage.

His mom had come to the rescue. Widowed a few years earlier, she had a spare annex in her house, and she would relish her son's company. They would be close to each other without being on top of each other. It was a Godsend. It was followed by a few other bright spots as his finances recovered: the liquidation of his business and the sale of his house raising some cash. In addition, he found some part-time work repping for an electrical manufacturer.

Things were looking up again.

Dennis and his mom found they enjoyed each other's company. On his birthday, she retrieved his boyhood coin collection from the attic and presented it to him. Dennis was delighted. The highlight of his collection were the old Lincoln wheat pennies from the first half of the twentieth century.

He now had the money to fill in some of the missing years and upgrade the condition of others. And now this rarity amongst rarities had found its way to him.

It seemed too good to be true. And, sadly, it was.

Closer inspection through the magnifying glass showed that a scammer had ingeniously taken a 1948 copper penny and filed down the left-hand side of the 8 to make it a 3.

A curiosity, worthy of a place in his collection, but of little value.

A few days later, a sales trip took him to Pittsburgh. Happily it gave him a chance to see his beloved Steelers in action against the Cowboys. Sadly they lost.

But after the game, to cool his disappointment, he dropped into an antique shop. There, he mentioned his particular interest in coins, and the owner asked if he would like to see a large collection that had just arrived. It was part of the estate of a local person. Its highlight was a magnificent collection of silver dollars,

so the $50,000 price tag was understandable, totally out of Dennis' league. But as a keen numismatist, he wanted to see it just out of interest.

As he looked through the collection he found a set of nickels, including one from 1913. When he took a closer look, his eyes nearly popped out of his head.

It was a Liberty Head. The rarest nickel of them all.

In 1913, Liberty Heads had been replaced by the Buffalo design. But a few years later an ex-employee of the Mint displayed five 1913 Liberty Head nickels at a numismatic convention. He claimed to have bought them, but it was generally assumed that he had struck them himself. Two of those nickels were now in private collections and three were in museums. But there had long been rumors of a sixth somewhere else.

And here it was, staring him in the face.

In numismatic circles, in any circles, it was priceless.

Dennis asked if he could buy just the nickels but was

told that the executors felt the owner would not have wanted to see the collection broken up. Dennis returned home and did some figuring. If he took all his savings, sold his car, and cashed in an endowment policy, he could raise $50,000, and the collection, including the 1913 nickel, could be his.

So, he did. And it was.

The deed was done.

Jesus pauses, takes a swig from his water bottle, and launches into his follow-up story:

. . . .

The waters rippled. The line trembled and tightened. The rod struck.

Parker Ryan was a high-flying PR executive. She had a silver tongue and a golden touch. Age 57, she now owned her own consultancy with a client list full of A-listers from the film and music industry. Unmarried, with a penthouse apartment near Central Park, her job was her life.

Except it wasn't her total life. Because she had a hobby that was very dear to her. She was an angler. More specifically, a carp angler. Even more specifically, a specimen carp angler. She pursued specimen carp with as much commitment and skill as she would pursue her next rock star client.

But whereas her aim with clients was to hang onto them for as long as possible, when it came to carp, she operated a strict catch, snap, and release policy. The walls of her room were adorned by photos of shiny live fish rather than stuffed dead ones.

Her hobby took her to all the top carp-fishing locations around the USA and Europe, the best of which were as expensive as skiing in Aspen and Méribel.

One weekend, she booked a B&B in Barkhamsted, Connecticut, a tranquil, bucolic spot set in a sprawling country estate.

There she hooked the biggest carp she had ever seen in her life. Not only had she hooked the carp, but the carp, lake, and its setting had hooked her.

On the spot she decided upon a complete life change. She wanted to be here, to fish this lake (which she suspected was bulging with prize carp), to enjoy this lovely spot, and to live a new lifestyle. But to do this, she would have to buy not just the lake but the massive mansion and countless acres that went with it.

If she sold her business, apartment, Bentley, and Ferrari it could all be hers.

So she did. And it was.

The deed was done.

The parables of the hidden treasure and the pearl

Matthew 13:44-46

44 "The kingdom of heaven is like treasure hidden in a field. When a man found it, he hid it again, and then in his joy went and sold all he had and bought that field.

45 "Again, the kingdom of heaven is like a merchant looking for fine pearls. 46When he found one of great value, he went away and sold everything he had and bought it."

So, what's this story saying to US, here and now?

What is your most precious possession?

Let's put it another way. If your house were on fire, what would be the first thing you would rescue?

We're talking about material objects here, not people, so the answer is not your children/spouse/parents/ grandparents/pet dog. It's not that they are not precious to you, simply that they are not the answer we want to the question we are posing!

Many people have said that the first thing they would seek to rescue would be their family photos. But as more and more of those become digital, scanned, and otherwise backed up on iCloud and OneDrive, it forces us to confront the question again.

We'll now widen it. What is your most precious or most desired possession? And what would you pay to replace it or gain it?

Ah, now it gets tricky, doesn't it? We start to feel grubbily materialistic. Mike and Ivan's thoughts are already spinning towards something red, with four wheels and a prancing horse logo.

But hang on a moment. Jesus talked about treasure and pearls. Those are pretty materialistic!

So, we'll ask again.

What is your most precious or most desired possession? And what would you pay to replace it or gain it?

Please try and give an answer. We'll wait a while and let you think.

There you go, not so difficult was it!

Or maybe it was. That doesn't matter. It's not the point.

Clearly, we don't know the answer. But we can tell you that, whatever it is, Heaven is worth far, far more.

Everything we have, in fact. That's what these two stories are saying to us, here and now.

We'll leave you alone again to think of the implications.

Reflection and prayer | What would I give to gain Heaven?

· ·

_____

_____

_____

_____

_____

What's this story saying to me, here and now?

· ·

_____

_____

_____

_____

_____

THE JOB APPLICATIONS

**Many fit the bill...but not all measure up.
Who will make the cut?**

"Well done people, let's break for coffee."

Two piles of paper sat on the desk, one considerably higher than the other.

Director of Human Resources, Megan Williams, addressed her team:

"So, we've reduced the applications from 115 to 17; and we've done that by being pretty ruthless in our assessment of their qualifications, experience, and character.

"But then this is a critical position we are trying to fill. The Head of Public Relations is the public face of the company. He or she will have no room for error due to the awful mistakes made over our recent product recall. Whomever we appoint must hit the ground running. We cannot afford to get this appointment wrong.

"Now comes the even tougher part of the exercise. These 17 applications need to be scrutinized again."

The team groaned inwardly but brightened at their director's next remark.

"But don't worry," she said, "I'll do it, here and now." The team then looked on amazed as she quickly sifted through the papers and sorted six into a pile on the right of the desk and 11 to the left. She then picked up the 11 and gave them to the team leader. "Here you go," she said. "You can put these with the other rejects, and we'll ask these six in for interviews."

She was heading back to her office when something in the atmosphere stopped her. She turned around and faced the puzzled faces.

"Ah, I guess you're wondering how I decided so quickly. It's quite simple, actually. We asked each applicant to name two CEOs whom they really admired. Three of those 11 gave just one name. They over-simplified the question. The other eight gave more than two names. They over-complicated it. Either way, they all ignored a clear brief, and that's an unacceptable trait in a senior PR person."

The parable of the net

Matthew
13:47-50

47 "Once again, the kingdom of heaven is like a net that was let down into the lake and caught all kinds of fish. 48When it was full, the fishermen pulled it up on the shore. Then they sat down and collected the good fish in baskets, but threw the bad away.

49This is how it will be at the end of the age. The angels will come and separate the wicked from the righteous 50and throw them into the blazing furnace, where there will be weeping and gnashing of teeth."

So, what's this story saying to US, here and now?

We do like Jesus' opening words in this parable:

"Once again…"

We can visualize him slapping his hand against his forehead, shaking his head, and sighing deeply in frustration.

He's frustrated that his disciples just don't seem to be getting the point, the point being that Heaven is not just for the privileged few. It's not an extension of any worldly class or caste system.

The parables of the Sower and the Weeds showed us that we shouldn't be selective about who we share the gospel with.

It's not our job to judge who we think is fit for Heaven and who isn't. That's God's job and he'll do it on Judgment Day, as the second half of this parable relates so vividly.

Which means that we all need to keep checking on how secure we are in our faith, especially as we know that Satan is doing his wily best to undermine it!

In the meantime, our job is to be fishers.

Fishers not anglers.

Anglers use a rod to try and catch a particular type of fish. And preferably a specimen one.

Fishers use a net to haul in as many fish as possible. This parable specifically refers to a net.

Our job is to bring the Kingdom close to as many people as possible.

To use a really, really big net and cast it as widely as we can!

Reflection and prayer | How wide am I casting my net?

· ·

_____

_____

_____

_____

_____

_____

What's this story saying to me, here and now?

· ·

_____

_____

_____

_____

_____

_____

THE WINE MERCHANT

Selling old world vintages...alongside new world varietals. Can they co-exist?

"I am sorry monsieur, but we do not sell American wines."

The customer looked puzzled.

"But we're having prime rib tonight, and I want to serve a big Napa Cab with it."

Claude gave a Gallic shrug of the shoulders.

"Ok, well what do you have in the way of Shiraz?"

"I am sorry sir, but we do not sell Australian wines either. Or South African, before you ask."

Now the customer looked annoyed. "Ok, I'll just have to go to Walmart."

"Yes sir, I think you should."

Claude Mignolet owns a wine shop in Louisville, KY. Or, as he would put it, the wine shop in Louisville. Since its opening, it has been stocked almost exclusively with French wines (although a thorough search of the premises may occasionally reveal a fine Barolo, Amarone, or Rioja).

Claude, like his father before him, has been a staunch believer that true wine comes only from the Old World.

His nephew, Pierre, has a job that requires him to travel extensively around the world. The job also comes with a generous expense account, giving him the opportunity to try fine wines from all parts of the world. He would often try to persuade Claude to stock at least a Napa Cabernet Sauvignon or a Marlborough Sauvignon Blanc. But Claude was having none of it.

Imagine then Pierre's shock, and delight, when he calls into the shop one day and finds it transformed.

As he enters the door he is presented with, to his left, a section signed as "Old World". The venerable French, Italian, and Spanish classics take pride of place here, and Pierre even spots a German Riesling.

To his right, he encounters "New World." Browsing the shelves here, he finds top vintages from the USA, Chile, Argentina, Australia, New Zealand, and a host of other countries. There is even an English sparkling white from Chapel Down.

"Uncle Claude, I'm amazed. What's happened?"

"My boy, I admit I am a traditionalist, but I am not as stuck in my ways as you may think. I have been carefully investigating these new wines for several years now and quietly building my cellars so that I can offer the best of the new alongside the best of the old."

Pierre continues to wander, amazed, around the shop. "Uncle, this is absolutely superb. I feel like I have died and gone to Heaven!"

The parable of the owner of the house

Matthew
13:51-52

51"Have you understood all these things?" Jesus asked.

"Yes," they replied.

52He said to them, "Therefore every teacher of the law who has become a disciple in the kingdom of heaven is like the owner of a house who brings out of his storeroom new treasures as well as old."

So, what's this story saying to  here and now?

Wine occupied quite a prominent place in Jesus' ministry and teaching, so we were keen to feature it in one of our rewired parables.

This one provided the perfect opportunity!

It's the eighth and last story in Jesus' "Heaven is like" series and, as verse 51 indicates, brings them all together.

What we particularly like about this story is the way that old and new exist harmoniously side by side. The new has not come to replace the old, and the old does not try to invalidate the new, a perfect change management scenario.

What Jesus seems to be saying here is that in Heaven everything will be brought together and reconciled. Past, present, and future: all believers across all countries, civilizations, and cultures, all relationships across family and friends, past, present, and future, a vast storeroom of treasures old and treasures new: Old World wines and New World wines.

A new Heaven and a new Earth, echoing Isaiah 65:17 and pointing towards Revelation 21:1.

What a powerful, exciting vision!

Reflection and prayer | What's my vision of Heaven?

· ·

_____

_____

_____

_____

_____

What's this story saying to me, here and now?

· ·

_____

_____

_____

_____

_____

It sure feels like Heaven to me!

If anyone is qualified to talk about Heaven, it's Jesus! After all, it's his home.

In these eight stories he takes us on a guided tour, peppered with personal anecdotes and insights. Those insights give us some tantalizing glimpses of what Heaven, the Kingdom of God, is like.

The parable of the weeds shows that it's worth getting excited about. Why else would the enemy, the devil, be trying to infiltrate it, pollute it, and prevent us from attaining it? (The parable also reassures us that the enemy will not penetrate Heaven. This is a place exclusively reserved for God and his friends. It's safe, and it's secure.)

The growing seed shows us how God is preparing an eternal future for us that is beyond our wildest dreams.

We really like the imagery of the mustard seed and the yeast. They present Heaven as a living organism, growing and expanding, and filling the world with its goodness.

The hidden treasure and the pearl reaffirm how precious Heaven is. Priceless, in fact. Something worth giving everything else up for.

The net encourages us to get actively involved in helping to fill Heaven by 'issuing invites' to all and sundry.

Taken together, collectively, these first seven stories start to build up a sense of the true Heaven in our hearts and souls rather than our minds.

The eighth story, the owner of the house, confirms and affirms it all. How great it is to know that come the day, we shall see a new Heaven and a new Earth as the two come together.

How great it is to know also that if we continue in our faith in Jesus, we are assured of a place there.

This is why Jesus is keen to give us a sense of what it will be like.

A final thought.

Have you ever had a wonderful feeling of peace, contentment, and fulfillment come over you? Maybe while sharing time with someone very close and dear to you; maybe prompted by a stunning sight of nature, a piece of music or art, or holding a new-born baby in your arms. Or maybe during a time of quiet, prayerful reflection.

It may be that, for those few moments, we experience a taste of Heaven.

And wow, isn't it good!

Jesus' ministry is now well into its stride.

His miracles are amazing people and his parables are challenging them.

Each one of this series of stories has a real cutting edge.

The Unmerciful Servant gives Peter an uncompromisingly blunt response to his question about how many times he should forgive someone who wrongs him (Plot spoiler alert: the answer is 'as many times as it takes for you to *really* do so, Peter.')

The story of the Good Samaritan would have staggered, confounded and almost certainly angered the 'expert of the law' to whom it was delivered.

The Places of Honor overturned the elitist societal norms of the day.

And Counting the Cost perversely and confrontationally dared his audience to follow him.

So, read on—and mark his words, if you dare!

   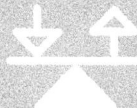  

THE TALE OF THE TWO DRIVERS

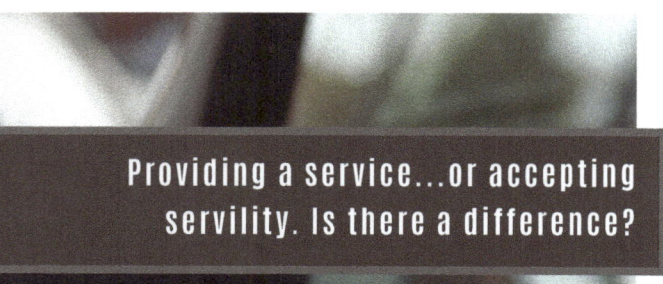

Providing a service...or accepting servility. Is there a difference?

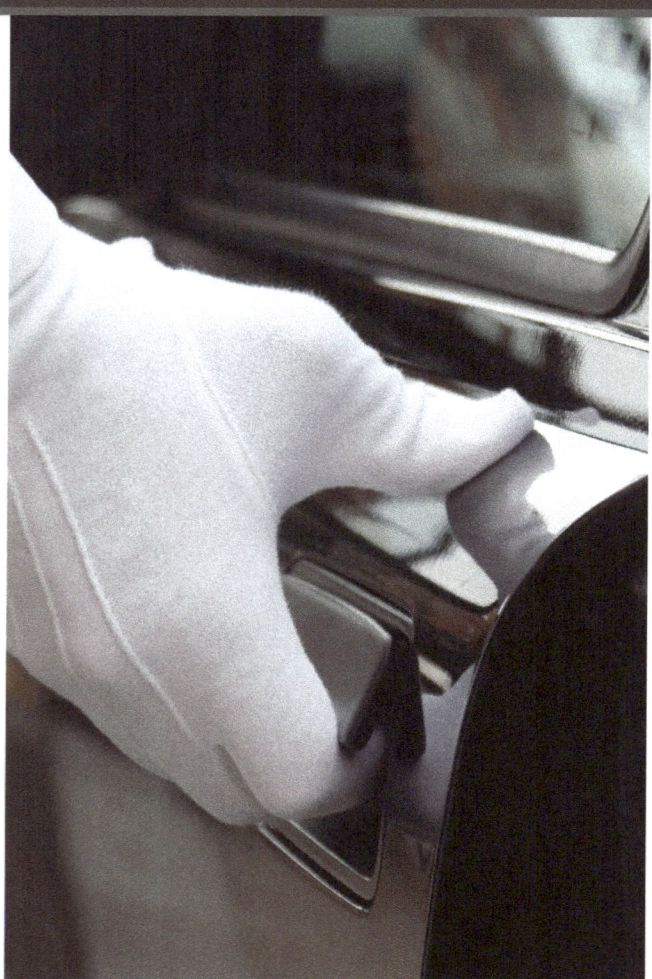

The disciples asked Jesus to increase their faith. In response, Jesus told them that if we trust in the faith we have, however feeble we may feel it to be, and use it, put it to work so to speak, even the seemingly impossible becomes possible. He also said to keep in mind who and what you are having faith in and why. Oh, and he told them this story:

• •

It was a cold night on Fifth Avenue. The wind howled from Central Park all the way downtown like a Siberian Express train.

A line of executive cars snaked along and around the curb side outside the Plaza Hotel's main entrance. A single figure occupied each, many wearing the peaked cap that still seems to be the obligatory mark of office for a professional chauffeur.

It had just turned midnight, but it would be another hour before their charges came boiling out of the hotel, looking for a fast ride home.

One of the drivers stepped out of his car and, tucking his head against the wind, walked down the line to a black Mercedes S-Class and knocked on the passenger door. Seeing him, the driver disabled the central locking and the man climbed in.

"Evening, Dwayne," said the driver.

"Hi Chuck. Heck of a night. I reckon it will be snowing within the hour."

"You could well be right there," Chuck replied. He pulled out a thermos flask. "Coffee?"

Dwayne gratefully accepted the steaming cup. "How's it going with you and your boss? He's a cold fish, isn't he? I've never seen him give you a word of thanks. Does he talk much in the car?"

"Not to me, no, but that's just his way. Mostly he's on the phone."

"Well, my guy is always chatting to me and asking about the wife and kids and what we're all up to. Got a good stock of jokes as well."

Chuck shrugged. "I guess my guy is just too focused on his job. As well as driving him, I run his wife around, pick the kids up from school, and wash their cars. I even do the shopping for them occasionally."

"You're kidding me!"

"Well, it takes all types. The way I see it, I'm there to make his life easier—that's my job. And as the saying goes, if a job's worth doing, it's worth doing well. Plus, if I look after his needs, I believe he'll look after mine. Incidentally, Dwayne, what's your rate of pay?"

"Forty dollars an hour. What's yours?"

"Sixty..."

The parable of the master and his servant

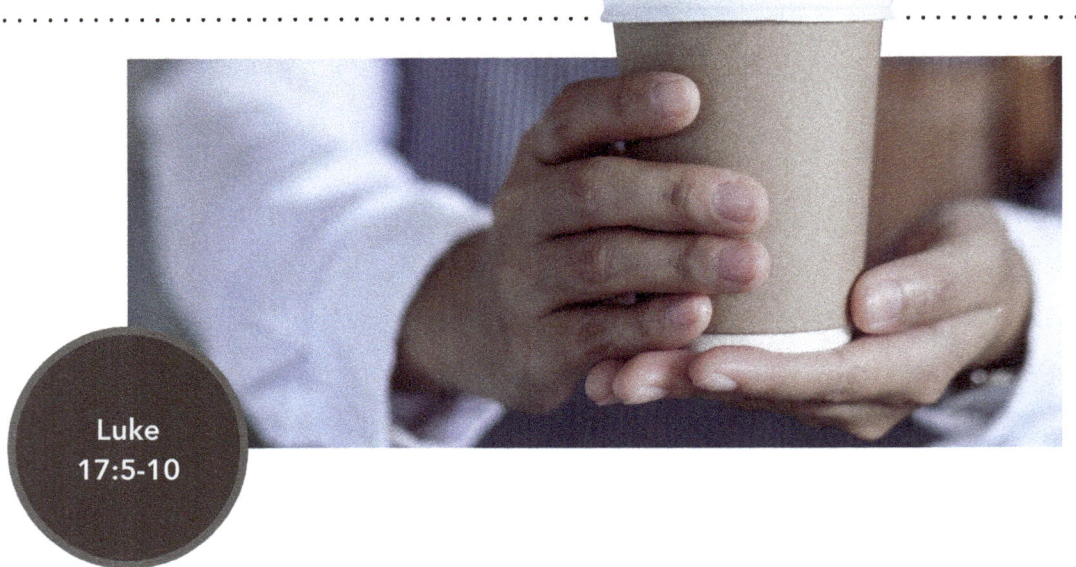

Luke
17:5-10

[5]The apostles said to the Lord, "Increase our faith!"

[6]He replied, "If you have faith as small as a mustard seed, you can say to this mulberry tree, 'Be uprooted and planted in the sea,' and it will obey you.

[7]"Suppose one of you has a servant plowing or looking after the sheep. Will he say to the servant when he comes in from the field, 'Come along now and sit down to eat'? [8]Won't he rather say, 'Prepare my supper, get yourself ready and wait on me while I eat and drink; after that you may eat and drink'? [9]Will he thank the servant because he did what he was told to do? [10]So you also, when you have done everything you were told to do, should say, 'We are unworthy servants; we have only done our duty.'"

So, what's this story saying to  US, here and now?

Most of us long for a very egalitarian culture, a democracy in which we all have equal stakes. This is fuelled by the media, allowing us to get up close and personal with famous people. It allows us to understand them better as people. And, like all people, they have their strengths and shortcomings.

In some ways, this exposure is a good thing. It instills greater accountability within those in a position of authority, and it can also make them appear somewhat more approachable.

But it does have some downsides. (The obvious one being invasion of privacy, but that is not the substance of this parable.)

It can generate an overfamiliarity between the public and authorities, which can breed a general lack of respect for institutions and individuals. We see this in pupil attitudes to teachers, public attitudes to law enforcement officers, and the way some professional athletes behave on the field.

Unwittingly, we can get a bit full of ourselves and develop an overblown sense of our own importance. The "me culture."

Our mindset is then that all authorities, be they government, local authorities, employers, banks, shops, even royalty in some countries, are there to serve us, not vice versa.

Consumerism rules. OK!

Maybe that is not entirely bad (a would-be dictator would hate it, for instance) provided it is kept in balance. But we do have to be extremely careful not to let it spill over into our relationship with God. That's what this parable addresses.

God loves us, encourages us to talk with him, and even sent his son to live among us as one of us. He wants an intimate relationship with us.

But he is also our Lord, our master, and our creator— the ultimate authority on earth and across time and space.

We must guard against intimacy becoming overfamiliarity.

Our prayer, praise, and worship, even at its most spontaneous and informal, must always be underpinned by a sense of awe and respect.

Critically, we must always be very clear on who is serving whom.

Our task is to serve God's agenda, not vice versa.

Jesus tells this parable to the apostles in response to their request that he increase their faith. In essence, he is telling them not to get carried away and be seduced by a sense of their own position and importance. They are there to serve God, and God has given them enough faith for all he wants them to achieve.

And so, it is with us. It is when we feel that we have really achieved great things for God that we can be at our most vulnerable.

It can breed within us too great a sense of our own holiness, or it can lead to a conditional, even contractual relationship: "I've done great things for you, God; now what are you going to do for me?"

We suspect that at some time or other, this happens to most of us. It certainly does to us. It has even happened in the course of writing this book.

So, if ever you catch yourself being a bit overfamiliar with God and taking liberties from the relationship, read this parable.

While the wages of sin are not particularly attractive, the wages of obedient duty are very good indeed.

So, take encouragement from Chuck. Faithful service that goes above and beyond the call of duty will bring its own rewards.

Reflection and prayer | Am I serving God's agenda?

· ·

_____

_____

_____

_____

_____

What's this story saying to me, here and now?

· ·

_____

_____

_____

_____

_____

THE CASE OF THE VINDICTIVE LANDLORD

To forgive...or be forgiven.
Which is harder?

Jesus was asked by Peter whether there was a limit on how many times we should forgive somebody. Anyone who has been persistently wronged by someone may feel this is a reasonable question. But Jesus told this story as a seemingly quite unreasonable response:

. . . .

Scene 1 | The phone call

"Oh no, you cannot be serious. There is no way you can cancel a lease because the tenant has missed just one month's payment. Look, he's a really good friend of mine. It's only $1000. I'll make the payment for him."

"Well, I am serious. I can cancel it, and I'm going to," the landlord replied. "I have a buyer who for some reason that I don't care about wants to pay stupid money for this house, and I can make a good buck on it. Fortunately for me, my tenant has defaulted, so he can go jump in a lake, and I can make a real killing. It's really touching that you want to make the payment, but it's too late. Maybe you can buy him an RV and move in with him as you're such good friends."

A mocking laugh ended the conversation, and the phone line went dead as he hung up.

Scene 2 | The inquest

Across town a lawyer steeled himself for a very tricky meeting with his boss Paul Croucher, the owner of Croucher Estates, a multi-millionaire who had built a

business from a one-room leasing property to a property empire that encompassed residential, commercial, and retail property development and leasing.

It would be a tricky meeting because a major error had come to light in the finance department.

As they had prepared to transfer the deeds on a large residential property, an assistant in the legal department had noticed that the mortgage borrower had been paying $660 per month rather than the $6,600 as stipulated in the contract. Someone had missed a zero! The upshot was that, over a 25-year mortgage term, the mortgage lender had been underpaid by nearly $1.8 million.

"Yes Paul, it's a major human error that occurred 25 years ago, and yes it should have been picked up at some point, so it's also a major systems error. We can't do anything now about the human error, but we can and already have amended the system to make sure such a thing can't happen again. Meanwhile, we have a cast-iron legal case for demanding that the underpayment be made before we transfer the deeds. This guy signed the original contract, and there is no way he cannot have known he was underpaying. We are within our rights to foreclose on him if we want. I say we get him in and have it out."

Scene 3 | The meeting

Later that day, Paul, the lawyer, and Brian Langford, the mortgage borrower, sat around a polished mahogany meeting table. The atmosphere was tense and adversarial. No coffee and cookies were being served. The lawyer laid out the case, culminating in a demand for an immediate payment of $1,782,000. To his surprise, Langford did not contest it. Instead, he burst into tears.

There followed an embarrassing few moments, and then Langford pulled himself together. "Look, I'm really sorry, but I'm a builder, not an accountant. I contract out all my financial administration, and they never said anything to me. I've spent 25 years building this business. I haven't the cash to make that size of payment, and I can't afford to lose that building. Either way, I would be bankrupted."

He appealed directly to Paul Croucher: "Have you never made a mistake that you regretted?"

Paul signalled to the lawyer and the two men left the room.

In his office he sighed. "Jack, I don't believe for a moment that he didn't know what was going on, and I can't stand the crocodile tears. But I do believe him when he says this would bankrupt him, and I don't feel comfortable forcing anyone out of business. Not only that, but our system really should have picked it up. Tell him we're going to write off the underpayment."

The lawyer went back into the meeting room and gave the news to Langford, who, amazed at his good fortune, left the building with a spring in his step and made a short journey across town to the local law courts.

Scene 4 | The showdown

Here a judge was due to pass judgment on the plea for unfair eviction that his tenant had brought against him. Langford received his second piece of unexpectedly good news that day as the judge ruled that, whilst unfair and verging on the immoral, the eviction was not in fact illegal and must stand.

As the tenant sat stunned, his friend arrived in the courtroom to comfort him.

It had taken Paul Croucher slightly longer to get across town, but he was still in time to see exactly who it was that was evicting his good friend. When Langford saw him, he did not even have the grace to look abashed. Instead, he gave a sardonic smile.

Paul's eyes bored deeply back into him as he reached into his pocket and pulled out his cell phone. Still holding his glare, he hit a speed dial. "Jack, about that huge underpayment we just decided to write off. A change of plan. Call in the debt. If the guy can't pay, we'll take all his business assets instead."

The parable of the unmerciful servant

Matthew 18:21-35

²¹Then Peter came to Jesus and asked, "Lord, how many times shall I forgive my brother or sister who sins against me? Up to seven times?"

²²Jesus answered, "I tell you, not seven times, but seventy-seven times.

²³"Therefore, the kingdom of heaven is like a king who wanted to settle accounts with his servants. ²⁴As he began the settlement, a man who owed him ten thousand bags of gold was brought to him. ²⁵Since he was not able to pay, the master ordered that he and his wife and his children and all that he had be sold to repay the debt.

²⁶"At this the servant fell on his knees before him. 'Be patient with me,' he begged, 'and I will pay back everything.' ²⁷The servant's master took pity on him, canceled the debt, and let him go.

²⁸"But when that servant went out, he found one of his fellow servants who owed him a hundred silver coins. He grabbed him and began to choke him. 'Pay back what you owe me!' he demanded.

²⁹"His fellow servant fell to his knees and begged him, 'Be patient with me, and I will pay it back.'

³⁰"But he refused. Instead, he went off and had the man thrown into prison until he could pay the debt. ³¹When the other servants saw what had happened, they were outraged and went and told their master everything that had happened.

³²"Then the master called the servant in. 'You wicked servant,' he said, 'I canceled all that debt of yours because you begged me to. ³³Shouldn't you have had mercy on your fellow servant just as I had on you?' ³⁴In anger his master handed him over to the jailers to be tortured, until he should pay back all he owed.

³⁵"This is how my heavenly Father will treat each of you unless you forgive your brother or sister from your heart."

So, what's this story saying to US, here and now?

Here's a tough question to ask ourselves, isn't it: "Have I ever wronged anyone?"

It's even tougher to digest the answer!

The fact is that most of us have wronged someone in our lives, even if by accident and unintentionally.

So, there is going to be someone whose forgiveness we need, for whatever reason.

The corollary of that is that there will be at least one person who needs our forgiveness, for whatever reason.

And all of us need, and have received, God's forgiveness of course.

We're not going to trivialize this topic by saying something like: "So we should all be forgiving."

The truth is that forgiving someone can be extremely difficult when that person has done you, or worse, someone close to you, some major wrong—harm even. We've each experienced that, and we're sure that many of you reading this will have too.

But this parable urges us always to consider how we should bestow forgiveness in light of the forgiveness we have received for ourselves: from others and God. Even if we find it beyond our capability to forgive now, we must continue to reflect and pray on it.

Because there is one further aspect we must take into account.

Unforgiveness is frequently accompanied by its twin sibling, bitterness. The object of that bitterness, the wrongdoer, is unaffected by it. The only person hurt by such bitterness is the person who holds it. In extreme cases, the victim of a wrongdoing can find him or herself being held prisoner by the bitterness he or she holds against the perpetrator.

We have heard more than one person talk of the sense of personal release, inner peace, and freedom experienced when, sometimes years after the incident, that person finally has been able to forgive and let go.

No wonder Jesus was insistent on the need to exercise forgiveness.

Reflection and prayer | Maybe I can't forget, but can I forgive?

. . . .

_____

_____

_____

_____

_____

What's this story saying to me, here and now?

. . . .

_____

_____

_____

_____

   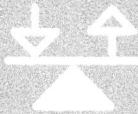  

THE CARING RUSSIAN ULTRA

You may not like him...
he may not like you, either.
But could you love each other?

The teachers of the law in Jesus' time were a persnickety bunch and constantly looking for a way of tripping Jesus up. They never succeeded, but that didn't stop them trying!

In this story, an "expert in the law" hoped to entangle Jesus in a definition debate: "When you say, 'love your neighbor,' who exactly is my neighbor?"

As always, Jesus came up with a stunning response:

· ·

A few years back, one of our mutual friends, Jermaine, got into a tough situation. Mike met him when they were both running in the Chicago Marathon, and Ivan met him on university business at Northwestern University, near Jermaine's house in Evanston, Illinois. At different times, both of us tried to turn Jermaine into a soccer fan, but he would have none of it. He was a Chicago Blackhawks fan. He loved the puck on the ice.

Jermaine was a high school sports teacher nearing the end of his career. At his retirement bash, the teachers, parents, and students all put their hands into their pockets, and together they bought him a plane ticket to the 2014 Winter Olympics in Sochi, Russia. Even better, they managed to get a ticket for the US vs. Russia game at the Bolshoi Ice Stadium. To say Jermaine was pumped would be an understatement. This was going to be a trip of a lifetime.

Jermaine flew from Chicago to Moscow and spent a couple of days looking around the city. Then, early in the morning of the US vs. Russia gameday, he flew to Sochi.

He met other US hockey fans on the way to the stadium. They were all nervous. This would be a real needle match. On the way to the game, the group popped into a restaurant for a quick bite. They were used to sky-high stadium food prices back home and wanted to save as much as possible for what they hoped would be a huge, postgame, celebration. After he had eaten, Jermaine went to use the restroom, and the other fans thought he had gone on ahead and left without him.

Jermaine came out of the restroom, realized he was on his own in a strange city, and headed to the stadium alone. He took what he assumed was a shortcut but ended up totally lost. Worse, he was suddenly surrounded by a mean-looking gang, who took one look at his American Hockey apparel and gave him a good kicking. Jermaine wasn't a big guy; he was built like a runner—tall and skinny. He was no spring chicken either. He was no match for the seven or eight guys who surrounded him, and they beat him badly. The gang stole his wallet, match ticket, passport, money clip, cell phone, and winter coat. He was left bloodied and cold on the street.

The police arrived on the scene but were worse than useless, and he only narrowly avoided being arrested. He remembers asking various people for help. A young couple, a businessman, some girls, even someone who appeared to be a priest. No one stopped to help. Maybe because they thought he was a dangerous hooligan. Maybe because they just didn't want to get involved. Perhaps they didn't understand English. Possibly, they were in too much of a hurry to get to the stadium (by now, it was getting close to faceoff.) Whatever the reasons, they walked on past, and Jermaine was becoming ever more cold, scared, and desperate.

He became even more alarmed when a shaven-headed, bare-torsoed, tattoo-engraved, iron-muscled, 250-pound monstrosity, draped in a Russian flag, arrived on the scene. It was freezing outside, and this nut job wasn't even wearing a coat. Jermaine's stomach churned as he realized this was the worst of the worst. A Russian ultra-nationalist, commonly known as an Ultra. These were out and out thugs, for whom extreme violence was the sport they loved, and any big event was an opportunity to embrace it. The gang who had beaten up Jermaine were like first-graders compared to this guy.

Fearing another kicking, or much, much worse, he tried to get away but was grabbed by the giant. To Jermaine's utter surprise, the guy sat him down and asked in broken English how he was. He gave him a drink (beer, not water, but Jermaine wasn't complaining)! He asked where Jermaine was staying, and on finding that Jermaine had lost all his money, passport, and cell phone, he hailed a taxi and took him to a nearby hotel. He persuaded the hotel owner, his friend, apparently, to find Jermaine a room, and left his own credit card as security. He then jumped back into the taxi to get to the game with a promise to return afterward. He did. Jermaine had no idea what he had gotten up to in the meantime.

But the question is: who was a neighbor to our friend?

The legal eagle who pressed Jesus thought long and hard and then hesitantly replied, "the Russian Ultra, because he had compassion."

"Absolutely! Take your lead from him!"

The parable of the Good Samaritan

Luke
10:25-37

²⁵On one occasion an expert in the law stood up to test Jesus. "Teacher," he asked, "what must I do to inherit eternal life?"

²⁶"What is written in the Law?" he replied. "How do you read it?"

²⁷He answered, "'Love the Lord your God with all your heart and with all your soul and with all your strength and with all your mind'; and 'Love your neighbor as yourself.'"

²⁸"You have answered correctly,"

Jesus replied. "Do this and you will live."

²⁹But he wanted to justify himself, so he asked Jesus, "And who is my neighbor?"

³⁰In reply Jesus said: "A man was going down from Jerusalem to Jericho, when he was attacked by robbers. They stripped him of his clothes, beat him and went away, leaving him half dead. ³¹A priest happened to be going down the same road, and when he saw the man, he passed by on the other side. ³²So too, a Levite, when he came to the place and saw him, passed by on the other side. ³³But a Samaritan, as he traveled, came where the man was; and when he saw him, he took pity on him. ³⁴He went to him and bandaged his wounds, pouring on oil and wine. Then he put the man on his own

donkey, brought him to an inn and took care of him. ³⁵The next day he took out two denarii and gave them to the innkeeper. 'Look after him,' he said, 'and when I return, I will reimburse you for any extra expense you may have.'

³⁶"Which of these three do you think was a neighbor to the man who fell into the hands of robbers?"

³⁷The expert in the law replied, "The one who had mercy on him."

Jesus told him, "Go and do likewise."

So, what's this story saying to US, here and now?

Jesus took the cozy concept of neighborliness, people we know, people we like, people nearby, people like us, and blew it wide apart.

Neighborliness, he said, is not about physical proximity; it's an attitude of mind, a relationship with humanity as a whole.

The Jews hated Samaritans with a passion. They were pariahs. Untouchables.

Jesus turned that prejudice against them.

We said that Jesus came up with a stunning response, and the law expert would indeed have been almost literally stunned. First, by the story, then by the logic that forced him to admit that a Samaritan had been a good neighbor.

We live in a world of 24-hour rolling news and global connectivity.

Never have we known our "neighbors" better. Do we allow that knowledge to confront our prejudices or just to confirm them?

It's an important question, because as Jesus points out in response to the law expert's first question, loving our neighbor is one of the keys to eternal life. And things don't get much more important than that!

Historical Footnote

It's possible to interpret the concept of a neighbor in two ways. In a metaphorical sense, any human being in need. And in a geographical sense, those physically closest to you.

In our hotwiring above, we've tried to link the two in a way that speaks to us today, here, and now.

But, when Jesus first told the story, it would have been radical teaching in both senses of neighborliness.

First, in Jewish culture, to suffer any kind of misfortune was regarded as a sign that you had sinned and incurred God's displeasure. The fault was yours, and the solution was to mend your ways. This story blows that apart. When he said, "Go and do likewise," Jesus was telling his audience, and us, that we need to look beyond any labeling of such people and instead see them as God's creation that he loves and cares about.

Second, the closest neighbors to the Jews in proximity were the Samaritans, the inhabitants of Samaria. In times gone by, this had been the Northern Kingdom of Israel, with Judah forming the Southern Kingdom. For various reasons, a deep rift had developed between the two.

In Jesus' story, a Samaritan shows love and compassion for a Jew. When he said, "Go and do likewise," Jesus was telling his audience to reconcile themselves with their closest neighbors, their ancestral brothers and sisters. To heal the family rift. He wanted them to go, in love for them, to make things right with them.

Where was the first recorded Christian church to be established outside Jerusalem?

Yep, in Samaria (see Acts 8).

As Peter and John hastened there to confirm the new Samaritan Christians with the Holy Spirit, maybe Jesus' parable was still ringing in their ears!

One final thought. Are you estranged from anyone whom Jesus may want you to make things right with? Maybe even someone you don't actually like very much?

Now could be your chance to make that right…

Reflection and prayer | Is God calling me to be a neighbor to someone, even if I don't like them?

· ·

_____

_____

_____

_____

_____

What's this story saying to me, here and now?

· ·

_____

_____

_____

_____

_____

THE PANICKING COLLEAGUE

In desperation...he asked for a big favor.
Was it an ask too far?

The disciples asked Jesus to teach them how to pray. In response, he taught them what we now know as "The Lord's Prayer."

He also told them a story:

· ·

An alarm blared through on the cabin speakers as the plane suddenly dropped like a rock.

It was pitch black; the cabin lights had failed.

The plane was depressurizing.

He reached out frantically to grab an oxygen mask but couldn't locate one.

The alarm continued to shriek.

Then his hand brushed the clock radio and fastened upon the phone.

Cal fought his way up and through the dark blanket of tiredness and disorientation.

The alarm lit up: 2:03 am.

As the phone rang again, he cursed inwardly and tried to clear his head.

As he did so, he realized he wasn't still on the plane.

A vicious summer storm had delayed his departure from Frankfurt. Four hours in the plane on the tarmac followed by a 10-hour flight. He had finally arrived home in Denver just before 1:00 am and, jet-lagged, had gone straight to bed.

He pressed the answer button, yawning.

"Cal, Cal, I'm so sorry to wake you, but I need you to email me the Global, Inc. sales pitch." It was his friend, Tom, a colleague from the office.

"Tom, it's 2:00 am. My wife and kids are—make that were—asleep, and I've had just one hour's sleep myself. What's the panic? The meeting isn't until Wednesday."

"No, no! I've just heard that the client is arriving tomorrow and wants to meet right away. I don't have a copy of the presentation on my system."

"Yeah, well, it will keep until morning. Please don't ring back. You'll wake my wife and kids again." With that, Cal pressed the end call button.

Cal hadn't even got back into bed before the phone rang again.

"I'm so sorry, Cal," Tom whispered. "I must have that presentation. Our next year's book of business depends on—

Cal abruptly ended the call and switched off his phone.

"Who was that honey?" his sleepy wife asked.

"Shhhhhh." Cal rubbed her shoulder. "Go back to sleep." She did.

Cal went back to bed. He tried to sleep, but jet lag was kicking in. He cursed Tom.

"You may be my close buddy," he muttered, "but that was way out of order." As he lay there though, other thoughts started running through his head. Poor guy must be really stressed... He probably wants to get himself fully rehearsed... It took a lot of guts to make those calls.

With that he slid quietly out of bed, padded downstairs to his computer, and emailed the document.

Before he went back upstairs, he sent a text to Tom: It's in your inbox. I'd have called you to say it's on the way but I didn't want to wake your wife and kids.

The parable of the friend in need

Luke
11:1-13

[1]One day Jesus was praying in a certain place. When he finished, one of his disciples said to him, "Lord, teach us to pray, just as John taught his disciples."

[2]He said to them, "When you pray, say:
"'Father,
hallowed be your name,
your kingdom come.
[3]Give us each day our daily bread.
[4]Forgive us our sins, for we also forgive everyone who sins against us.

And lead us not into temptation.'"

[5]Then Jesus said to them, "Suppose you have a friend, and you go to him at midnight and say, 'Friend, lend me three loaves of bread; [6]a friend of mine on a journey has come to me, and I have no food to offer him.' [7]And suppose the one inside answers, 'Don't bother me. The door is already locked, and my children and I are in bed. I can't get up and give you anything.' [8]I tell you, even though he will not get up and give you the bread because of friendship, yet because of your shameless audacity[he will surely get up and give you as much as you need.

[9]"So I say to you: Ask and it will be given to you; seek and you will find; knock and the door will be opened to you. [10]For everyone who asks receives; the one who seeks finds; and to the one who knocks, the door will be opened.

[11]"Which of you fathers, if your son asks for a fish, will give him a snake instead? [12]Or if he asks for an egg, will give him a scorpion? [13]If you then, though you are evil, know how to give good gifts to your children, how much more will your Father in heaven give the Holy Spirit to those who ask him!"

So, what's this story saying to  **US,** here and now?

When you haven't got a prayer, pray.

It's amazing how even people who eschew God will instinctively endorse prayer when seeking to comfort others:

"I'll say a prayer for you."
"You're in our thoughts and prayers."
"Please God, things will get better."

We see it too when times of national and international crisis result in a spike in calls to prayer and even church attendance. The Cuban missile crisis, the death of Princess Diana, 9/11, Covid-19. It's almost like an internal default switch is thrown within the national psyche.

"When you haven't got a prayer, pray."

Hotwiring that line could lead to a powerful call to prayer advertising campaign. It would start where people are at, address a need, and offer a clear benefit. "When you haven't got a prayer, pray!" There are worse ways to find a way to God.

Of course, we hardened Christian prayer warriors may turn up our noses and say something like "prayer should be the first thing you use, not the last."

But sometimes, even for us, it can get difficult.

Maybe we're disinclined to approach God because we feel the issue is too trivial. Does God really care that my goldfish is unwell? Or maybe we fret that we don't know the right way to ask or can't find the fine words that will get us God's attention and consideration.

The point of friendship is that we don't have to stand on ceremony, don't have to find exactly the right words, and don't have to worry that it will all be too trivial.

Even if our friend thinks any or all these things, they'll help simply because we've asked, because our friends love and care about us.

God loves and cares about us, too.

It's not the manner of asking him that's important, it's the act of asking.

Reflection and prayer | When I haven't got a prayer, what do I pray?

· ·

_____

_____

_____

_____

_____

_____

What's this story saying to me, here and now?

· ·

_____

_____

_____

_____

_____

_____

A DRAMATIC NIGHT
AT THE OSCARS

When hubris and humility looked each other in the eye. Who blinked first?

We all know people who are overly full of themselves. Jesus told this story especially for them:

. . . .

At the very front table in the room, the famous young actor smiled. Held court. Savored the atmosphere. Sipped the fine champagne. Smiled at the cameras. Relished the attention. Graciously acknowledged those around him.

How he loved being center stage. How he loved his admirers. And they him. This was going to be his moment and his alone.

"The Oscar for Best Actor goes to…"

He rose. He froze.

At the very back of the room sat an aging Slav actor.

He froze. He rose.

The spotlights swiveled. The cameras hunted.

The old man walked the length of the room.

As he reached the front, he glanced left.

Two pairs of eyes engaged.

Humility met humiliation.

Humiliation blinked.

The parable of the place of honor at the wedding feast

Luke
14:7-11

7When he noticed how the guests picked the places of honor at the table, he told them this parable: 8"When someone invites you to a wedding feast, do not take the place of honor, for a person more distinguished than you may have been invited. 9If so, the host who invited both of you will come and say to you, 'Give this person your seat.' Then, humiliated, you will have to take the least important place. 10But when you are invited, take the lowest place, so that when your host comes, he will say to you, 'Friend, move up to a better place.' Then you will be honored in the presence of all the other guests. 11For all those who exalt themselves will be humbled, and those who humble themselves will be exalted."

So, what's this story saying to US, here and now?

You are who you are.

This little story is of massive relevance to us today.

It flies like an arrow to the heart of our culture.
A culture that lauds success.

A culture in which being self-made is the highest accolade:

What you are is more important than who you are.

But no company or team or army is 100% composed of high-flyers.

High-flyers must accept that one day someone will fly higher than them.

Who you are is as important as what you are.

Our media are tuned into and turned on by success, in business, sports, and politics.

We live in the age of celebrity: movie, music, and Tik-Tok stars, as well as social media influencers. But the media also love to debunk a celebrity whose ego has outgrown their mojo.

How they are is more important than what they are.

Once in a while, someone emerges whose celebrity seems to stem from their humility and integrity: Gandhi, Mother Theresa, Nelson Mandela, Queen Elizabeth, Keanu Reeves.

How they are is as important as who they are.

Such people also exist in every state, city, town, and local community.

They are hard to find because they don't big-up what they do.

Instead, they work quietly behind the scenes in hospitals, care homes, local charities, community groups, and churches. In years gone by, they'd have also gone to war, prepared to sacrifice their lives in service to their country.

How they are defines who and what they are.

They are our volunteers, the unpaid and often unsung heroes of our age.

If you are lucky enough to know one, why not try and find a way to show him or her your appreciation?

Reflection and prayer | Who do I really admire?

. . . .

_____

_____

_____

_____

_____

What's this story saying to **me,** here and now?

. . . .

_____

_____

_____

_____

THE FREE LUNCH

When those who think there's no such thing...get to miss out on the best meal ever. What was on the menu?

A lot of eating and drinking goes on in the Bible. Here's a story about a feast that Jesus told while at the dinner table:

. . . .

The human volcano that was Aldo Cabrera threatened imminent eruption:

"How dare they insult me like this. It is a personal insult. I cannot, will not, accept it," said the angry chef.

The waiters, wisely, kept a discreet distance from the pyroclastic cloud.

Aldo was one of Mexico's preeminent chefs, with a string of restaurants, signature dishes, and cookbooks to his name.

Excited by the number of gringos that queued nightly to get into his restaurants in Cancun, Playa del Carmen, and Puerto Vallarta, he was about to open a restaurant in Toronto.

Acting on a suggestion from his marketing manager, he had invited food critics and journalists to a private preview lunch the day before the official opening.

That day had now arrived.

But Aldo had just been informed that most of those invited had not bothered to reply to the invitation, and all those that had done so had declined, citing a variety of prior engagements and family commitments. The pick of the bunch was a journalist who had just received the delivery of his new Porsche 911 GTE and, forgoing the lunch, was driving it to the Toronto Motor Sports Park for a track day.

Like many creatively endowed people, Aldo's talent was accompanied by a tempestuous personality, and in his case, one with a distinctly Latin flavor.

So, the answer "nobody" to his query about how many were likely to come caused Mount Aldo to finally blow his top.

"It's an insult," he roared. "A personal insult. In Mexico they would be clamoring for a place at one of my tables; yet here I have nearly 50 meals that will go to waste."

Miraculously, the lava flow stopped as a smile spread slowly over his face. "I have an idea," he said. "My food may not be good enough for the pampered paparazzi, but it will certainly be appreciated by those who have nothing."

He singled out three waiters: "You, you, and you, go and round up the homeless people in the local area." "Yes, boss," they said, "but we're unlikely to find 50 of them at this time of day." Aldo summoned two other waiters. "Then you and you go to the hospital and invite patients, doctors, and visitors. Include taxi drivers if need be.

"I want my restaurant to be packed this lunchtime with people who appreciate and enjoy it.

"And Alan," he said, grabbing his hapless marketing manager by the lapels, "you make sure that none of those ungrateful press reptiles can enter any of my restaurants. Anywhere, ever."

The parable of the great banquet

Luke
14:15-24

[15]When one of those at the table with him heard this, he said to Jesus, "Blessed is the one who will eat at the feast in the kingdom of God."

[16]Jesus replied: "A certain man was preparing a great banquet and invited many guests. [17]At the time of the banquet he sent his servant to tell those who had been invited, 'Come, for everything is now ready.'

[18]"But they all alike began to make excuses. The first said, 'I have just bought a field, and I must go and see it. Please excuse me.'

[19]"Another said, 'I have just bought five yoke of oxen, and I'm on my way to try them out. Please excuse me.'

[20]"Still another said, 'I just got married, so I can't come.'

[21]"The servant came back and reported this to his master. Then the owner of the house became angry and ordered his servant, 'Go out quickly into the streets and alleys of the town and bring in the poor, the crippled, the blind and the lame.'

[22]"'Sir,' the servant said, 'what you ordered has been done, but there is still room.'

[23]"Then the master told his servant, 'Go out to the roads and country lanes and compel them to come in, so that my house will be full. [24]I tell you, not one of those who were invited will get a taste of my banquet.'"

So, what's this story saying to US, here and now?

When Mike worked as an ad agency CEO, his schedule was always full.

Lots of meetings, sometimes meetings about meetings.

On one ridiculous occasion, he realized he was in a meeting about a meeting about a meeting.

The gaps between the meetings were also full: mainly meetings with food. He would have breakfast, lunch, or dinner scheduled each day. On many days, breakfast, and lunch, and quite frequently, breakfast, lunch, and dinner.

Ivan's schedule was much the same. When he served as a university president and was visiting alumni across the USA, he often had two breakfasts, an early lunch, a late lunch, afternoon tea, dinner, and supper. Every person he met was important to him, and he wanted to ensure that they all felt special.

So, for Mike and Ivan, there were more meals than you could shake a stick at! Mike ate with clients, colleagues, suppliers, journalists, prospective employees, and heads of rival agencies. Ivan ate with his administrative cabinet, alumni, elected officials, donors, other university presidents, foreign dignitaries, journalists, students, and parents.

Such busy schedules meant that they were both booked weeks in advance.

Sometimes a lunch had to be rearranged because of an emergency, or another appointment needed to be scheduled with a greater priority. But sometimes, they would look at the next day's appointments, and their hearts would sink. What seemed like a sensible appointment scheduled eight weeks earlier now looked like a complete pain in the behind! Maybe it was unfortunate timing. Or maybe it was when Mike or Ivan felt dog-tired and needed time for themselves.

Either way, they had other things that needed to be done or things they'd prefer to be doing, like watching Tottenham Hotspur or the St. Louis Cardinals.

What to do?

When they got weary, Mike and Ivan sometimes tasked their assistants to postpone a meeting or ask a colleague to deputize for them. Neither liked doing this. But sometimes, they simply ran out of gas.

When they had to postpone a meeting, both felt a pang of guilt.

So, this parable resonates with them.

In another parable, Jesus spoke about a great banquet to which the invited guests simply did not arrive. In this parable, the invited guests at least made excuses.

In our rewiring, the journalists' assistants earned their salaries that day, sending apologies and excuses, some genuine, others certainly fabricated.

But in Jesus' story, the invitation to the meal is an analogy for his invitation to us to follow him.

This invitation is far more important than any business or social meeting. It's more important than a meeting at the White House, an event at Carnegie Hall, or even, and we know you can hardly believe this, a VIP tour of Busch Stadium, St Louis.

Jesus invites us to a life-changing, life-securing meeting. There is nothing more important, nothing that should cause us to decline, postpone, or cancel the invite.

If you've been hesitating or procrastinating, or know someone else who has, make sure that the invitation to meet with Jesus is accepted pronto.

Reflection and prayer | How can I 'squeeze Jesus in?'

. . . .

_____

_____

_____

_____

_____

What's this story saying to **me,** here and now?

. . . .

_____

_____

_____

_____

_____

THE TALE OF THE
NO-GOOD DO-GOODERS

High on promise...low on delivery.
How low did they go?

When we commit ourselves to Jesus, we need to understand what a commitment it is, as these two un-compromising stories make clear:

· ·

The door opened, and the wind howled by. From this height, the curvature of the earth was clearly discernible. Gaps in the clouds afforded glimpses of the ground 5,000 feet, nearly one mile, below.

Terrified, Mo froze. This hadn't been in the script, certainly not when he had woken up one sunny morning after a good night on the town in Phoenix and thought to himself: "I want to do a skydive."

A lot of his buddies had done one, and dined out on the experience afterwards, so it couldn't be that difficult.

And it wasn't. One phone call to the local cancer charity had them chomping at the bit. They would organize everything. All he needed to do was gather sponsors and turn up on the day.

Getting sponsored was not a problem. Mo had lots of well-connected and well-heeled friends. He came from a large family, none of whom was short of a buck or two. So, the money poured in. When he told the charity that pledges had topped $25,000 they were ecstatic.

It didn't stop there. Hannah, his administrative assistant, organized a "see Mo di(v)e" barbecue and party at the airfield. With tickets priced at $100 a pop, sales quickly topped $7,500, with more expected on the big day.

For once in his life, Mo felt really good about himself.

But now, as he recoiled from the gaping void below, all he felt was fear.

It was a tandem dive, so his dive-partner was behind him. His partner's voice came over the intercom: "Come on Mo, just let go and step back out of the plane."

But Mo refused to budge. This one small step was a giant leap too far, something he had not expected, and something he knew he could not commit himself to.

"I can't do that. You'll have to drag me out."

"Sorry," said the instructor. "We're not allowed to. It has to be your decision."

"Well, I'm also sorry," said Mo, "but my decision is that there's no way I am going to step out of this plane until it is sitting on the ground."

And so, the plane returned with Mo still firmly ensconced within it.

His friends were not impressed. His assistant quit. His family was embarrassed. The charity had to kiss goodbye to a donation likely to have topped $35,000.

Apart from her embarrassment over Mo's non-jump,

Hannah, by now his ex-assistant, had a different problem. Inspired by Mo, she had, on the spur of a moment, decided to pursue a girlhood dream to be part of a four-woman bobsleigh team doing the famed Cresta run in St. Moritz, Switzerland. It turned out that three of her friends were winter sports fanatics and shared the same dream. As two of them were teachers, they all decided it would be best to do it during the Christmas break.

So, Hannah had snapped into action, obtained details of flights and hotel, and enrolled them at a nearby gym that had a partnership arrangement with a ski resort that specialized in training people for winter sports.

They commenced a grueling 12-week fitness program and attended weekly lectures from an Olympic bobsledding medal winner.

At the end of the program the four girls came together over a meal to review plans. Hannah opened proceedings. "So, guys, where are we at?"

"Well, we've booked our flights and hotel for the whole of the Christmas break," her three friends replied. "What day are we doing the run?"

"Gosh, you certainly are eager beavers aren't you," laughed Hannah.

"No, just sensible," came the reply. "It's a holiday week, so flight and hotel availability will be limited and very expensive if you leave it too late. Have you not booked yet?"

"Um, no, actually," came the reply.

"Well, that was dumb. It cost us $2,500 each, booking in advance. You'll probably have to pay double that now. And what date have you booked the run for?"

"Errrr," said Hannah. "Do you need to book it? I thought you just turned up and waited your go."

"Of course you need to book it! It's in high demand and not cheap at the best of times. Probably about $1,000 each for a three-run routine."

"Whaaat!" shrieked a horrified Hannah. "That means I'll have to spend at least $3,000, maybe closer to $5,000. That's all my life savings."

"Well, it's also your life dream. It's ours as well, which is why we've already forked out."

"Noooo," Hannah shrieked again. "No way am I going to do that. I need that money for my wedding and house deposit. I'm sorry, but you three will have to do it without me."

"Hannah," they replied, "the three of us can't do that."
 "Why not?"

"The clue's in the name, you airhead. It's a four-woman bob."

"Well, find someone else," countered Hannah.

"That's impossible at this stage. You have to do it with us."

"Well, I can't, and I won't. I'm as disappointed as you. I'm sorry because I know I'm letting you down, but I'm mostly letting myself down, which in many ways is worse."

"No, it's not, you deluded knucklehead. You are mostly letting us down. It's not going to cost you a penny. We're the ones who are going to lose out big time once we've paid the cancellation fees on flights and hotels.

"Not to mention also losing out on our dream.

"All because you won't honor your commitment."

The parable of counting the cost

Luke
14:25-33

²⁵Large crowds were traveling with Jesus and turning to them he said: ²⁶"If anyone comes to me and does not hate father and mother, wife and children, brothers, and sisters—yes, even their own life—such a person cannot be my disciple. ²⁷And whoever does not carry their cross and follow me cannot be my disciple.

²⁸"Suppose one of you wants to build a tower. Won't you first sit down and estimate the cost to see if you have enough money to complete it? ²⁹For if you lay the foundation and are not able to finish it, everyone who sees it will ridicule you, ³⁰saying, 'This person began to build and wasn't able to finish.'

³¹"Or suppose a king is about to go to war against another king.

Won't he first sit down and consider whether he is able with ten thousand men to oppose the one coming against him with twenty thousand? ³²If he is not able, he will send a delegation while the other is still a long way off and will ask for terms of peace. ³³In the same way, those of you who do not give up everything you have cannot be my disciples.

So, what's this story saying to US, here and now?

The invitation to follow Christ is freely and unconditionally given. "Come as you are" is the invitation. Acceptance is also easy. There is no complicated and long-winded application system. No interview to prep for. No references to provide. The decision to follow Christ is a lifesaving, life-gaining one.

But it's also a life-changing one and not one to be taken on a whim, or fad, or flight of fancy, It's a real commitment.

It challenges and changes lifestyle priorities.

On the surface, it may seem a small step, but it is a huge leap with big consequences: "those of you who do not give up everything they have cannot be my disciples." Having invited Jesus into our life, we then need to be prepared to turn that life over to him.

As Captain James T. Kirk would (ungrammatically) put it, "to boldly go," even to the point of jumping out of a perfectly good airplane or blowing our life's savings.

But the prize is huge: the achievement of our real-life dream, our eternal-life dream.

Reflection and prayer | Am I boldly going?

. . . .

_____

_____

_____

_____

_____

_____

What's this story saying to me, here and now?

. . . .

_____

_____

_____

_____

_____

_____

This set of seven parables concludes the first phase of Jesus' storytelling.

In the 19 parables contained in this first volume, *'Stories Without Spin'* he has taught on a wide variety of topics in a way that amazed people, because they had never heard teaching like this before.

Jesus would often conclude his stories with a simple injunction: 'those that have ears, let them hear.'

Or as we have paraphrased it: 'Mark my words.'

He has used his storytelling technique to really connect with people. To get their attention and cause them to consider many aspects of their ancient faith through a new spiritual lens.

He has also used his storytelling to open the minds and souls of his 12 closest disciples. And in so doing has given them a technique that they themselves could use. It's likely that Peter, James, John and the rest would have found themselves retelling these parables. Maybe even rewiring them to suit particular circumstances.

People are flocking to see Jesus. To hear Jesus. And maybe even, in desperation, to touch Jesus. Those that do so in faith find their lives transformed.

But others are not loving what they are seeing and hearing. They are also desperate to get their hands on Jesus, but for entirely different reasons.

Along the way Jesus has upset quite a few very influential and powerful people.

People who form the religious and state establishment.

They feel threatened.

And when the establishment finds itself threatened it bites back.

So Jesus adapts his storytelling to get his bite in first.

In *'Volume 2: Stories With Bite'*, you can continue to walk alongside him as he ups the ante by throwing incendiary stories onto the flames.

Stories that would tie his opponents in knots.

Stories that would pave the way towards his ultimate storyline of crucifixion, death, and resurrection.

Afterword

Jesus told his parables to a wide range of audiences and for a variety of purposes.

He told them to his small band of disciples to encourage and train them; to vast crowds to inform and inspire them; as guidance to those genuinely seeking enlightenment; to hostile groups such as the Pharisees to chastise them; and as a riposte to scheming opponents and their efforts to discredit or entrap him.

As we've been writing this book, we've found ourselves thinking time and again about the effect the parables would have had on these varying audiences.

Would they have been intrigued? Challenged? Shocked? Encouraged? Stunned? Confused? Informed? Bewildered? Enlightened? Annoyed? Enthused? Angered? Affirmed?

All of the above.

What they would not have been is bored or disinterested.

Our aim has been to help people of today experience those parables afresh, whether hearing them for the first time or the umpteenth.

We hope that, as you've read them, you've tried to stand in the shoes of those various audiences, to project yourself into their mindsets, and that you've also tried to visualize Jesus, with all his human passion and spiritual power, standing in front of you, talking directly to you.

If not, go back and read some of them again, not our "rewirings," but the originals, as Jesus told them. That's why we've included them.

As with all scripture, we should expect the parables to speak to us today. We hope that, in our commentaries, we've touched on some ways in which they do this.

Clearly, we do not know all of you readers, individually and personally. So, we haven't been able to tailor our messages to each and every one of you. But Jesus does know you, intimately. And if you give him the time and space to do so, he will tell you precisely what these parables mean for you.

Finally, Jesus told his parable stories so they could be shared with and retold to others, particularly to those who couldn't or wouldn't come and hear them from him firsthand.

So, if you know someone who doesn't yet know Jesus, and they are someone who you feel Jesus wants to speak with, please share this book with them so he can do so!

May the grace of our Lord Jesus Christ, the love of God, and the fellowship of the Holy Spirit be with you all (2 Corinthians 13:14) now and for evermore. Amen.

Mike, Ivan and Jason

. . . .

Biographies

Mike Elms has more than 40 years' experience in business, marketing and advertising. As UK CEO of two major ad agencies, Ogilvy & Mather and Tempus Group plc, he has worked with a wide range of blue-chip companies at C-Suite level, including: Unilever, Nestle, Ford, Mercedes, Chrysler, DHL, Shell and Guinness. He has also advised a wide range of Christian organizations. An experienced church leader and preacher, he is Board Chair of Lògòs Foundation, a Christian charity focused on using advertising and PR to advance the Gospel.

Ivan Filby is the President and CEO of Seedbed, a subsidary of Asbury Theological Seminary. He has had a distinguished career in higher education and has a Ph.D. in Management and an MA in Evangelism. He taught at The University of Dublin: Trinity College for sixteen years before moving to the USA to chair the Management Department at Greenville University. He is the author of *Livestream: Learning to Minister in the Power of the Holy Spirit* and *Speak Tenderly: Prophetic Ministry Seasoned with Grace.*

Jason Moore has created the original artwork for *Jesus Unbranded* using his unique skill to combine the use of AI with his own artistic sensibilities.

Inside Mike's mind: 'Unbranding Jesus'

During my time as an adman I've encountered a whole bunch of brands that have lost their way and strayed from their original purpose or mission.

A succession of marketing regimes may have added, subtracted, or, in a variety of ways, 'tinkered' with the product or service itself.

A succession of advertising executives may have tried to make their mark by putting their own stamp and 'spin' on the brand messaging.

And so the brand ends up in a very different place from which it started.

Over the years I have discovered that the only remedy is to strip all that 'baggage' away and go back to the brand's roots. To rediscover the original purpose and proposition that made it great in the first place. To see, understand, and respect the original, authentic brand. And then allow it to speak for itself again.

I've given that stripping away process a label. I call it 'unbranding.'

Over the centuries Jesus has been constantly interpreted and reinterpreted. Some things have been added, others lost.

Some people and organizations have sought to hijack Christianity, and even Jesus himself, to use them to serve their own agenda. For reasons good and bad. Let me stress, I'm simply observing here, not judging.

As Ivan and I pursued our Mission of 'Keeping the stories alive', we realized something deeper was occurring. We found ourselves standing among his audience, hearing him speak directly to us. We listened intently to every parable he told. And by placing them in chronological order, we got to travel with him throughout the whole of his ministry.

Through the lens of the stories he told, we came face to face with the original, authentic, unadulterated Jesus.

Such is the power of the parables.

So our mission became to let them speak for themselves again.

As you immerse yourself in them, our prayer is that you too will find yourself standing in the awesome presence of the original, authentic and 'unbranded' Jesus; and that you will hear him speaking directly to you, here and now.

Mike

· ·

Inside Ivan's mind: 'Writing in the Spirit'

Any author will tell you that a blank sheet of paper is a very intimidating thing indeed.

Only your creativity can put ink on paper; writer's block is always lurking just around the corner.

But once pen is put to paper, the creative juices begin to flow.

Mike and I discovered that being presented with many sheets of paper full of the words of Jesus, together with a divine instruction to re-imagine them, is *infinitely more intimidating.*

Who were we to even contemplate that?

But once we made a start we discovered that time after time, story after story, the Holy Spirit was inspiring us.

Many a time we looked at each other after a completed rewiring and asked: 'where on earth did that come from?'

The answer was, of course, nowhere on earth.

Mike does not have a degree in theology. But he does have a passionate and abiding love of Jesus. As an ordained minister I was happy to become the mind to his heart, and together, I believe we made a pretty good team.

Our aim was to ensure our theology was sound but not 'in-your-face'. So, we avoided terms such as Sanctification, Incarnation, Absolution and even Salvation. But whilst the words may not be there, the concepts they encapsulate most definitely are. Because they are baked into the parables.

Rewiring the storylines was only the half of it, though.

We then had to discern what each parable is saying to us, here and now.

Again we sought to strike a balance between theology and readability.

What is the eternal, spiritual theme that each of these every day, worldly storylines has embedded within it? There too the Spirit inspired us. What we have written was his message to us.

But he may, no make that *almost certainly will*, have a different message for each of you.

We urge you to let him inspire you also. As you hear Jesus speaking to you through his parables—our words or his own—ask the Spirit to reveal what the words have to say to you, here and now.

And if the Spirit gives you another storyline, don't be afraid to grab a blank piece of paper and start writing!

Ivan

. . . .

Inside Jason's mind: 'Seeing is believing'

AI, Artificial Intelligence, is a topic that stirs emotions.

Some see it as a bright new future: a huge opportunity for the world.

Others as a dark menace: an existential threat to mankind.

As always, reality lies somewhere between these two extremes.

Mike and Ivan observed to me that if we had named it for what it actually is—Automated Information—it would be a whole lot less scary.

I liked that.

(They are also very keen to emphasise that the only AI involved in rewiring the parables was Authors' Insights powered by Amazing Imaginations!)

Let's be clear. AI is a tool. But tools can be used for good or for evil. A screwdriver is a tool. It can be used to put up a shelf or construct a bomb. A Kalashnikov AK47 is also a tool. It can be used to maintain law and order or commit acts of terrorism.

AI can be used for either good or evil. As can music, literature, photography and so on.

Speaking personally, I use it in a design and illustration context and I like to think I wear a white hat!

I use AI as the starting point: it helps me to begin to bring a concept to life.

But I have to then input my own artistic and design skills. And use other techy tools to get the concept to look just the way I want it to look. No, let me rephrase that: to get the concept the way Mike and Ivan want it to look.

Their minds, guided by the Spirit, have created a fresh vision, a verbal picture, for each of the parables. My job has been to understand that vision and bring it to reality by turning it into an arresting image.

And there you have another way of expressing AI: Arresting Images.

Arresting Images powered by Artistic Inspiration.

In Jesus' day, stories were told in words, to be retold and handed down, generation to generation.

In our day, we are more visually attuned. If Jesus were telling the parables now, he'd almost certainly have some visual aids.

Because, these days, a single, striking image is worth a thousand words.

But please—don't tell Mike and Ivan!

Jason

www.ingramcontent.com/pod-product-compliance
Lightning Source LLC
Chambersburg PA
CBHW041137120626
46547CB00020B/3021

* 9 7 8 1 9 6 3 2 6 5 3 1 6 *